Network Neutrality and Digital Dialogic Communication

T0225644

In the months after the Federal Communications Commission's (FCC) 2017 decision to repeal network neutrality as US policy, it is easy to forget the decades of public, organizational, media and governmental struggle to control digital policy and open access to the internet. Using dialogic communication tactics, the public, governmental actors and organizations impacted the ruling through YouTube comments, the FCC online system and social network communities. Network neutrality, which requires that all digital sites can be accessed with equal speed and ability, is an important example of how dialogic communication facilitates public engagement in policy debates. However, the practice and ability of the public, organizations and media to engage in dialogic communication are also greatly impacted by the FCC's decision. This book reflects on decades of global engagement in the network neutrality debate and the evolution of dialogic communication techniques used to shape one of the most relevant and critical digital policies in history.

Alison N. Novak is an Assistant Professor of Public Relations in the College of Communication and Creative Arts at Rowan University. She received her PhD from Drexel University in Communication, Culture, and Media. Her work explores the intersections of policy, media discourses and public engagement. She is the author of *Media, Millennials, and Politics: The Coming of Age of the Next Political Generation* and the coeditor of *Defining Identity and the Changing Scope of Culture in the Digital Age*. Her work is featured in *Wired Magazine* and *Redbook Magazine*, and on NBC News.

Melinda Sebastian is an Assistant Professor of Communication Studies at Kutztown University. She received her PhD from Drexel University in Communication, Culture, and Media. Her research focuses on gender, technology, law and policy. She recently published "Privacy and Consent: The trouble with the label of 'Revenge Porn'" in *Feminist Media Studies* and has a book chapter entitled "The Digital Age and the Social Imaginary" in *Remembering and Forgetting in the Digital Age, Law, Governance, & Technology* for Springer Verlag, arriving in 2019. She is the Secretary Historian for the Feminist Division of the International Communication Association.

Routledge Studies in Media Law and Policy

The Press Clause and Digital Technology's Fourth Wave
Media Law and the Symbiotic Web
Jared Schroeder

Network Neutrality and Digital Dialogic Communication
How Public, Private and Government Forces Shape Internet Policy
Alison N. Novak and Melinda Sebastian

Network Neutrality and Digital Dialogic Communication

How Public, Private and Government Forces Shape Internet Policy

Alison N. Novak and Melinda Sebastian

Routledge
Taylor & Francis Group

LONDON AND NEW YORK

First published 2019 by Routledge

2 Park Square, Milton Park, Abingdon, Oxfordshire OX14 4RN

52 Vanderbilt Avenue, New York, NY 10017

Routledge is an imprint of the Taylor & Francis Group, an informa business

First issued in paperback 2020

Library of Congress Cataloging-in-Publication Data
A catalog record has been requested for this book

ISBN: 978-1-138-31775-8 (hbk)
ISBN: 978-0-367-60678-7 (pbk)

Typeset in Times New Roman
by codeMantra

Contents

Figures

Acknowledgments

Both authors would like to thank the colleagues, faculty and administration of their institutions: Rowan University and Kutztown University. The project emerged from years within the doctoral program in Communication, Culture, and Media at Drexel University. The authors are grateful for the support from Drexel faculty and friends. Specifically, Dr. Myles Ethan Lascity's editing and watchful eye shaped the first draft of this book. Dr. Rachel M. Magee's friendship and collaborations continue to inspire this project. Finally, both authors would like to thank the editors from Routledge and the Taylor & Francis Group for their guidance.

Alison would like to thank her parents, Michael and Denise Novak, for their support and encouragement throughout this project and life. Greg Richter and the Richter family's insights have also greatly shaped this project. In addition, Alison appreciates the ongoing support from Leon Boulanger, Melinda Novak, Jerry Meyers, Dorothy and Edward Markowski and Carol MacMullen. She is grateful for guidance from colleagues, advisers and friends, including Ernest Hakanen, Julia Richmond, Julia Hildebrand, Sherri Jean Katz, Wajeeha Malik, Alicia Rosali and Emad Khazraee.

Melinda would like to thank her mother, Winifred Moran Sebastian Esq., for her help and support on this project and all others. Her advice is always the best, and so is she. Melinda would also like to thank her adviser, Dr. Wesley Shumar, Professor of Communication at Drexel University, for his guidance and support. She again highlights her friend, Dr. Myles Ethan Lascity, Assistant Professor of Journalism at Southern Methodist University, as his input shaping this book was invaluable.

Introduction to Network Neutrality and Dialogic Communication

On an overcast December day in 2017 in Washington, D.C., the Federal Communications Commission (FCC), led by Chairman Ajit Pai voted to repeal network neutrality.[1] While shocking for many around the world, the decision came after decades of political, corporate and public debates regarding the regulation of the world's most powerful communication medium: the internet. The 2017 decision impacts nearly every facet of the internet and has the potential to dramatically change every day digital life for global users. In the wake of these important changes, it is easy to identify the 2017 decision as a conclusion to the network neutrality debate and overlook the decades of engagement and political progress that surround the issue. However, this would be a mistake: many important lessons regarding the co-construction of public policy, digital dialogic communication and challenges to traditional policy development process must be drawn to better inform our understanding of how communication can shape public policy in the digital age. Further, because the elimination of a network neutrality policy can significantly impact the communication potential of the internet, it is important to examine how this potential evolved through the debates of network neutrality.

Network neutrality is defined as a policy that supports a free and open internet devoid of paid differences in service access and availability. Until December 2017, the United States and the majority of countries around the world operated under network neutrality, meaning internet service providers (ISPs) were not allowed to slow down or accelerate internet connections between users and specific websites. All digital content was delivered at comparable speeds based on the type and amount of data communicated, not the financial relationship of the website to the ISP. The FCC's 2017 decision to repeal network neutrality allowed ISPs to monetize connections and individualize connection speeds based on their relationship with the website.

Thus, ISPs could charge websites for faster delivery to a user, or slow down connections between users and websites who fail to pay the ISP (Figures A.1 and A.2).

For users, public advocates and some digital organizations, this repeal seemingly marked the end of a neutral era of accessibility for users to all websites. However, some large digital organizations and ISPs celebrated the repeal, issuing statements of appreciation for the FCC's decision and highlighting how organizational practices might change to better serve the public and reflect new policy. Within hours of the FCC decision, #NetNeutrality was trending on Twitter, physical protests began forming outside FCC headquarters and corporations around the world issued statements responding to the new policy changes. In short, the immediate aftermath reflected the evolution of tensions, responses and engagement with the network neutrality debate, cultivated over nearly four decades.

Arguably the most important feature of the network neutrality debate focuses on the internet as a communication medium. Communication scholar Bimber argues that a defining characteristic of the internet rests on its ability of users to communicate vital information with each other through the use of websites and platforms.[2] This is relevant for users around the world as the internet facilitates communication to and from global citizens. For example, Twitter facilitated communication during the 2012 Arab Spring, where protesting Egyptian citizens could connect and form protest plans.[3] Or, in 2017,

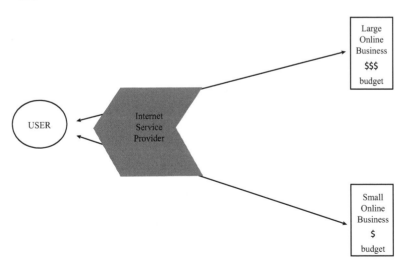

Figure A.1 Network neutrality diagram.

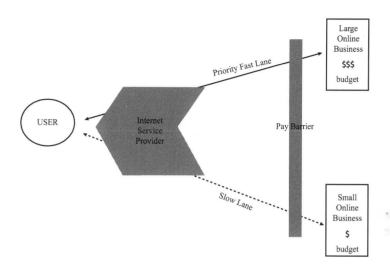

Figure A.2 Nonnetwork neutrality diagram.

when Puerto Rico was devastated by Hurricane Maria, images shared on Facebook motivated donations and relief efforts.[4] As Morris and Organ argue, the internet is a mass medium because of its communication potential and ability to elicit change in the public.[5] Any policy, such as network neutrality, that can slow down or prioritize specific messages or communication over others can dramatically shape public knowledge and ability to participate.

It was the internet's communication potential that was the focus of earlier lawsuits regarding network neutrality practices and public policy. A 2010 Netflix versus Comcast challenge perhaps best illustrates the importance of network neutrality's impact on the communication potential of the internet. In 2010, Comcast partnered with Blockbuster to challenge Netflix's stronghold of the digital video streaming market. While the partnership did not last, in 2014, Comcast charged Netflix additional fees to maintain high streaming quality and undisrupted service for users. Netflix argued that this was a violation of network neutrality and posited that Comcast was not allowed to discriminate against access to the Netflix site.[6] Netflix's initial rejection of Comcast's higher fees led to users experiencing a slowing down and lower quality of Netflix streaming services.[7] Meanwhile, Comcast's lawyers argued that Netflix should pay higher fees since streaming accounted for such a high percentage of the data used on its network. In order to fix streaming quality issues and prevent customer outrage,

Netflix reluctantly agreed to pay the higher fees and instead turned to the FCC for support.[8] Netflix branded this issue as "interconnection," launching what was called a "public relations war" against Comcast's new fees. Scholars and journalists argued that taking on the largest ISP in North America was a risk, especially for an organization whose bottom line rested on its ability to effectively digitally communicate programming with customers.[9] The risk paid off, and in 2015, the FCC announced that it was ready to listen to Netflix's arguments on interconnection as a violation of network neutrality.[10]

What hung in the balance of Netflix's dispute with Comcast was the communication potential of the internet. CNET found that from October 2013 to March 2014, the speed and quality of Netflix programming declined by 27%, meaning customers experienced greater technical difficulties at an alarmingly high rate.[11] Some readers may even remember this era for the emblematic spinning circle against a black backdrop as Netflix endlessly buffered content. In a nutshell, this is the impact of eliminating network neutrality: user access to digital content is mediated by the financial relationship of an organization to the ISP, not the availability of information.

A 2015 ruling by the FCC agreed that interconnection fees were a violation of network neutrality and other non-streaming organizations voiced that discriminatory fees were a challenge to business's ability to communicate with the public.[12] Two years later, when the FCC reconsidered network neutrality in 2017, mental health organizations joined Netflix's protest and argued that a decision to repeal the policy could affect countless lives (beyond frustrations about low entertainment streaming quality). In a *Medium* article that outlined risk of slower connection speeds between mental health digital hotlines and vulnerable individuals, contributor Sledge argued that "seconds matter when you're dealing with the difference between life and death."[13] A repeal of network neutrality could especially impact mental health nonprofits who cannot afford to pay faster interconnection fees. These organizations rely on network neutrality for quick and effective communication. For example, when someone posts a suicidal message on a community forum, organizations have just minutes to respond, call police and send help. Slower connection speeds may inhibit this process and reaction times. A repeal of network neutrality would allow an ISP to charge mental health organizations a premium for faster connection speeds, which are necessary in its effort to offer help.

Another organization who advocated for keeping network neutrality was the popular third-party review site, Yelp. The multinational organization provides a digital space for customers to post reviews of recent business transactions. These reviews and comments give potential customers valuable information when making future purchasing decisions. Yelp reviews can positively and negatively impact a business's reputation and profits. Recognizing that slower connection speeds may inhibit Yelp from providing these reviews to future customers, the site released a July 2017 statement outlining its support for keeping network neutrality and supporting public dialogue within third-party review sites.[14] Yelp particularly advocated that network neutrality aligns with Yelp's mission of helping small businesses achieve digital presence, particularly those too small or early in their lifespan to pay for faster internet connection.

Yelp is also a prime example of a platform that facilitates digital dialogic communication, a theory that also defines network neutrality's impact on the communication potential of the internet. Digital dialogic communication explains how digital platforms such as Twitter or Yelp provide a space for customers to provide feedback to organizations and for organizations to respond to feedback through dialogue. On Yelp, this means organizations can post reply messages to customer reviews (publicly or privately), adapt business practices to incorporate customer suggestions and form digital communities of customers as they relate to the organization. A policy of network neutrality means that these digital dialogic practices can take place at equal speed, providing all organizations with equal opportunity to engage the public. Hypothetically, a repeal of network neutrality means that smaller organizations who are unable to pay for faster connections (aka internet fast lanes) cannot garner this same feedback and will have a diminished opportunity for digital dialogic communication.[15] It could also mean that an ISP like Comcast could start its own third-party review site and slow down access to competing sites like Yelp to encourage users to switch platforms. A repeal of network neutrality inserts barriers in the digital dialogic communication process and would therefore challenge Yelp's ability to facilitate this dialogue.

Public relations theorists Kent and Taylor originally identified digital dialogic communication as a valuable process that produces dialogue between organizations and the public.[16] The World Wide Web's critical capability facilitates communication and valuable feedback which can be used to improve organizational processes and "negotiate ideas and opinions."[17] For example, universities use digital dialogic communication practices by responding to questions posted by prospective students in online forums (some controlled by the University and some public forums on third-party websites).[18]

Digital dialogic communication can happen within a number of digital spaces including organizational websites, social media platforms and third-party review sites like Yelp. Organizations identify invaluable public feedback within these spaces and public relations practitioners rely on this information to adjust organizational messaging, strategies and practices.[19]

Dialogic communication is considered an ethical approach to decision-making, one that hallmarks an era of two-way symmetrical communication relationships between an organization and stakeholders.[20] Similar to the Habermasian theory of the public sphere, dialogic communication allows members of the public to engage and participate in decisions that hold direct implications for daily life.[21] Organizations are encouraged to authentically listen to public feedback and use digital spaces to engage in dialogue, rather than historical one-way asymmetrical communication that focuses on dissemination instead of dialogue as the key to relationship management.[22]

In addition to Yelp's earlier concerns that a repeal of network neutrality may inhibit smaller businesses from two-way communication, digital dialogic communication is an important part of the network neutrality debate. Because many organizations have critical interest in all global rulings on network neutrality, countless groups have turned to digital dialogic communication to engage the public and garner public support. For example, Yelp asked users to provide feedback on network neutrality in their July 2017 statement. The announcement included links for users to provide Yelp with feedback, links for users to post on the FCC official commenting system and links for users to write Congress through *Battleforthenet.com.* Yelp, similar to other large digital organizations, sought to motivate the public to use digital dialogic communication and engage relevant actors. The hope was that an onslaught of public comments and messages would motivate organizations to engage in a dialogue with these stakeholders which may ultimately sway organizational support in favor of network neutrality. In short, Yelp not only saw digital dialogic communication as potentially impacted by a repeal of network neutrality, it also saw digital dialogic communication as a way to fight and advocate for the policy. This dual role of digital dialogic communication is at the heart of this book: a study of both how network neutrality impacts digital dialogic communication and how digital dialogic communication impacts the network neutrality policy formation process.

Other instances of digital dialogic communication as an advocacy strategy include John Oliver's viral segments on network neutrality in 2014 and 2017. In these segments, Oliver starts with a humorous explanation of network neutrality followed by an impassioned cry for his audience to comment (and sometimes troll) the online FCC commenting system to demonstrate support for the policy. Oliver's segments was not only hailed for overwhelming the FCC with more public comments than expected and crashing the system, but also with galvanizing public support of the policy and impacting the favorable 2015 FCC decision.[23] Although the FCC did not directly respond to every comment within the system, analyses from *Time* and *The Washington Post* argued that the comments did get the attention of FCC Chairman Tom Wheeler and helped shape the written portion of the FCC decision in 2015.[24,25] These digital dialogic initiatives demonstrate the effect the process can have on policy decisions.

Because large media organizations like Yelp, Comcast and Netflix have high stakes in network neutrality, they spend billions of dollars on lobbying efforts to impact policy development around the world. These lobbying efforts are again a type of dialogic communication that takes place between organizations and governments. Through (often critical) media coverage of these lobbying efforts, the public too has attempted to impact policy through digital and physical protests such as public comments on the FCC commenting system. Again, this public demonstration is a type of dialogic communication that takes place between the public and the federal government. Thus, dialogic communication is not only directly impacted by network neutrality policy but also used by public, organizational and governmental forces. It is fundamentally important to study how these forces use dialogic communication, as well as how network neutrality policies may impact dialogic communication in the future.

The debate over network neutrality is not the only policy tension that uses digital dialogic communication in the policy development process. In addition, network neutrality is far from the only concept that organizations spend billions of dollars attempting to regulate. Another poignant and familiar concept, free speech, as protected by the first amendment, was historically positioned by scholars as aligned with network neutrality, and decisions on the policy could hold lasting impact on free speech in the digital age.

It is the salience and timeliness of the network neutrality debate that demands critical insight into how digital dialogic communication has impacted the policy development process. In the wake of the 2017 FCC ruling to repeal network neutrality, it is important to look at the historical role and process of dialogic communication and how it may be used (again) to influence policy decisions around the world.

Notes

1 Chris Hayes, Evelyn Farkas, and Chris Matthews, "ALL IN for December 14, 2017, MSNBC." *All in with Chris Hayes*, 2017.

2 Bruce Bimber, "The Internet and Citizen Communication with Government: Does the Medium Matter?" *Political Comsmunication* 16, no. 4 (1999): 409–428.

3 Khayrat Ayyad, "Human Rights Organizations' Use of the Internet as a Communication Medium in Egypt." *Journal of Arab & Muslim Media Research* 5, no. 2 (2012): 167–185.

4 Chris Grahm, "'Rough! Rough! Rough!': Dominica Prime Minister Posts Dramatic Facebook Updates as Hurricane Maria Destroys His Home." *Telegraph.Co.Uk*, September 19, 2017. www.telegraph.co.uk/news/2017/09/19/roof-gone-dominica-prime-minister-describes-fury-hurricane-maria/.

5 Merrill Morris and Christine Ogan, "The Internet as Mass Medium." *Journal of Communication* 46, no. 1 (1996): 39–50.

6 Mathew Ingram, "Here's Why Comcast Decided to Call a Truce with Netflix." *Fortune*, July 5, 2016. http://fortune.com/2016/07/05/comcast-truce-netflix/.

7 Dara Kerr, "Netflix's Hastings Makes the Case for Net Neutrality." *CNet*, March 20, 2014. www.cnet.com/news/netflixs-hastings-makes-the-case-for-net-neutrality/.

8 Jacob Minne, "Data Caps: How ISPs Are Stunting the Growth of Online Video Distributors and What Regulators Can Do about It." *Federal Communications Law Journal* 65, no. 2 (2013): 233.

9 Jon Brokin, "Netflix Says It Will Pay Tolls to ISPs Not Just Comcast." *ArsTechnica*, March 20, 2014. https://arstechnica.com/tech-policy/2014/03/netflix-says-it-will-pay-tolls-to-more-isps-not-just-comcast/.

10 Jon Brokin, "Netflix, Call Your Lawyers, FCC Is Ready for Interconnection Complaints." *ArsTechnica*, February 27, 2014. https://arstechnica.com/information-technology/2015/02/netflix-call-your-lawyers-fcc-is-ready-for-interconnection-complaints/.

11 Jon Brodkin, "Netflix Performance on Verizon and Comcast Has Been Dropping for Months." *ArsTechnica*, February 10, 2014. https://arstechnica.com/information-technology/2014/02/netflix-performance-on-verizon-and-comcast-has-been-dropping-for-months/.

12 Brian Fung, "Remember Netflix's Deal with Comcast? The FCC's Proposal on Net Neutrality Could Overturn Agreements like Those." *The Washington Post*, February 4, 2015. www.washingtonpost.com/news/the-switch/wp/2015/02/04/remember-netflixs-deal-with-comcast-the-fccs-proposal-on-net-neutrality-could-overturn-agreements-like-those/?utm_term=.e65911d402e8.

13 Benjamin Sledge, "The Repeal of Net Neutrality Will Cripple Mental Health Offices." *Medium*, December 6, 2017. https://medium.com/@benjaminsledge/the-repeal-of-net-neutrality-will-cripple-mental-health-f0af144d7423.

14 Yelp, "Yelp Stands Up for Net Neutrality." www.yelpblog.com/2017/07/yelp-stands-net-neutrality.

15 Yelp, "Yelp Gives Net Neutrality Five Stars." www.yelpblog.com/2015/02/yelp-gives-net-neutrality-five-stars.

16 Michael L. Kent and Maureen Taylor, "Building Dialogic Relationships through the World Wide Web." *Public Relations Review* 24, no. 3 (1998): 321–334.

17 Ibid., p. 325.

18 Joye Gordon and Susan Berhow, "University Websites and Dialogic Features for Building Relationships with Potential Students." *Public Relations Review* 35, no. 2 (2009): 150–152.

19 Wonsun Shin, Augustine Pang, and Hyo Jung Kim, "Building Relationships through Integrated Online Media: Global Organizations' Use of Brand Web Sites, Facebook, and Twitter." *Journal of Business and Technical Communication* 29, no. 2 (2015): 184–220.

20 Sheila M. McAllister-Spooner, "Fulfilling the Dialogic Promise: A Ten-Year Reflective Survey on Dialogic Internet Principles." *Public Relations Review* 35, no. 3 (2009): 320–322.

21 Nicholas Browning, "The Ethics of Two-Way Symmetry and the Dilemmas of Dialogic Kantianism." *Journal of Media Ethics* 30, no. 1 (2015): 3.

22 Michael L. Kent and Maureen Taylor, "Building Dialogic Relationships through the World Wide Web." *Public Relations Review* 24, no. 3 (1998): 325.

23 Mike Snider and Elizabeth Weise, "John Oliver May Have Helped Spur 15000 Comments to FCC on Net Neutrality." *USA Today*, May 9, 2017. www.usatoday.com/story/tech/talkingtech/2017/05/09/john-oliver-may-have-helped-spur-150000-comments-fcc-net-neutrality/101480100/.

24 Soraya Nadia McDonald, "John Oliver's Net Neutrality Rant May Have Caused FCC Site Crash." *The Washington Post*, June 4, 2016. www.washingtonpost.com/news/morning-mix/wp/2014/06/04/john-olivers-net-neutrality-rant-may-have-caused-fcc-site-crash/?utm_term=.f97c6ac1be6b.

25 Victor Luckerson, "How the John Oliver Effect Is Having Real-Life Impact." *Time*, July 10, 2015. http://time.com/3674807/john-oliver-net-neutrality-civil-forfeiture-miss-america/.

1 Overview of Network Neutrality

In a 2017 article from *Medium,* Simon reflected on the historical and current truth behind network neutrality:

> The fight over net neutrality is one of the most important political debates America is facing at the moment...And yet, there is one odd thing. Type "Net Neutrality" into your search bar and you will inevitably get a variation of one particular article as a result: The *'Why you should care about net neutrality'-piece.*[1]

Simon's reflection is correct; the internet is filled with thousands of articles that attempt to convince the public that network neutrality is a critical issue for 21st-century citizens. Beyond these cries for civic attention, the articles also suggest that there is a culture and history of citizen apprehension and ambivalence toward the regulatory topic. Although there are groups of involved and engaged citizens, the overall conclusion is that network neutrality, although important, is largely removed from public attention. Perhaps this backdrop illustrates the mandate to research and understand the moments of engagement throughout the network neutrality debate. Their perceived rarity (by journalists) encourages the examination of other forces, such as organizations, regulators, journalists and elected officials, in the network neutrality debate and how they shape contemporary policy. In addition, if there is a perception of a disengaged public, this suggests a need for scholarly attention to engagement, in the form of digital dialogic communication practices. Dialogue involves a desire for communication and adjustment from both participating parties. If one party is disengaged (or perceived as disengaged), then the ability to form a true dialogue may be challenged, as sociologist Eliasoph described the hesitation of public involvement in politics or policymaking.[2]

A large deterrent to public engagement rests on the perception that public policy is unapproachable and largely handed down from government elites. However, as Weible, Sabatier and McQueen argue, this perception of elitism is faulty, and in reality, most public policies are co-constructed by a number of actors invested in the process, including members of the public.[3] Thus, public policy is a construction of the values of government, public, media and organizational interests.[4] In many ways, construction and dialogue resemble each other: they both rely upon the involvement of multiple audiences, authentic listening and the mutual adjustment of policy goals.

Construction of public policy is important for a number of reasons. First, it allows all stakeholders to provide feedback and shape policies for favorable outcomes.[5] This produces greater investment in policy decision-making and implementation.[6] For example, in Canada, parliamentarians allowed citizens, organizations and media outlets to provide feedback on proposed trade policies in an effort to minimize backlash when policy was finalized. For parliamentarians, the construction process gave all parties a greater sense of investment, thus improving the quality and acceptance of the finalized policy.

Second, input from various stakeholders allows policymakers to generate informed decisions with greater evidence. For example, the Netherlands and Sweden invited scientists to contribute to policy task forces before drafting and proposing policy that would regulate these industries.[7] Finally, policymakers also found a greater acceptance of policies from the wider public when stakeholder input is used in the creation process. Even in countries where policy is heavily controlled by state actors, such as China, the acceptance and ease of implementation of digital policies were greatly improved when policy was formed after discussion with stakeholders.[8] Even when the co-construction is an illusion, policymakers who frame policy as a product of co-construction benefit.

The "co-construction of public policy" and "public policy development theories" originate from sociological work on social constructivism.[9] Within this framework, policies are the product of many voices, interests and perspectives contributing to larger discursive trends and structures.[10] Public policy is not a product of one political elite making decisions but rather a reflection of many stakeholders who impact the decision-making process. For example, a policymaker might meet with members of an impacted community, lobbying groups representing affiliated organizations, media analysts, political strategists and party/political leaders all before designing, proposing or implementing public policy. DeGrasse-Johnson identified this process when examining national dance policy in Jamaica, which produced greater acceptance of the policy once it was implemented.[11]

Policy constructionists argue that even when policymakers attempt to build policy in isolation without the input of various stakeholders, they still rely on information and ideas discursively constructed by these parties.[12] It is impossible to escape the constructed world; thus, all policy decisions reflect some input from stakeholders. The degree of this input, and who gets the most voice in the process, is dynamic and changes based on the cultural and historical contexts of an issue.[13] In four decades of network neutrality policy development and evolution, various stakeholders have dominated the construction process, arguably all but controlling policy decision-making at different points in time. This chapter examines the stakeholders responsible for the policy control of network neutrality over four time periods, reflecting on the digital dialogic strategies used by each group.

Co-construction involves a dialogue between parties as they attempt to make decisions and plan strategies. Elwood and Mitchell emphasize that dialogic relations must take place in policy development, particularly when there are many stakeholders involved in the process.[14] Using Habermas's theory of the public sphere, the authors argue that the internet is a new public sphere, allowing stakeholders to engage in "autonomous rational debate about the future."[15] In the new digital public sphere, dialogic communication allows the stakeholders to present arguments that will shape a policy such as network neutrality. These arguments become the foundations for policies as they are formalized through regulatory processes, such as lawmaking.

Kent and Taylor posit that organizations benefit from digital dialogic communication because it provides feedback from stakeholders on key policy and business issues.[16] Similarly, governmental and regulatory officials benefit from digital dialogic communication because it provides information from the public on proposed legislation and strategic actions. While theories of digital dialogic communication have primarily focused on the relationship between an organization and its public audience, similar dialogic tendencies are observed in other parts of the policymaking process.

The key notion of digital dialogic communication builds from the public relations grand theory of "two-way communication" or using the internet to facilitate communication between an organization and the public. While there is some difference between dialogue and two-way communication (discussed later), this communication system appears in other places within the policymaking process, including between lobbyists and regulators/government officials, between journalists and organizations, and between countries. Two-way communication, facilitated through digital spaces, occurs between all stakeholders in the policy development process. As noted by Taylor and Kent, this communication can be a type of engagement with other stakeholders and the policy issue itself. Figure 1.1 illustrates how various stakeholders might engage each other to create policy.[17]

In this model, all stakeholders have the potential to engage each other, often using the digital space for this exchange. For example, the public engages in communication with the Federal Communications Commission (FCC) through the online commenting system. Linklater argues that communication does not need to result in a direct reply to every online comment.[18] Instead, a transformation of policy or perspective by the FCC (even the very slightest) demonstrates that dialogue occurs from digital dialogic practices. Digital dialogic communication is not just a conversation of words between an organization and an audience but part of a desire for the mutual adjustment of behavior, strategy or initiatives that includes perspectives shared during two-way communication.[19] It involves listening to the other party and integrating feedback into decisions.[20]

There is ongoing criticism of the equation of dialogue with two-way communication (which this text aligns with).[21] Dialogue requires two-way communication, but not all two-way communication is dialogue. Dialogue involves a genuine and ongoing attempt to integrate

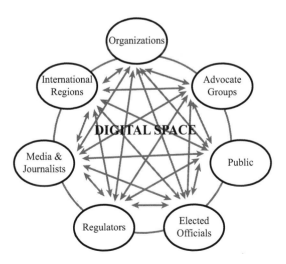

Figure 1.1 Diagram of dialogic stakeholders.

stakeholders into decision-making, while two-way communication, in public relations scholarship, requires communication to take place between stakeholders and the public.[22] While this theoretical debate persists, evidence for two-way communication and dialogue as sometimes separate and sometimes overlapping systems appears throughout the network neutrality debate.

There is further ongoing debate of the value of dialogic communication and the "emancipatory potential" it provides for all stakeholders.[23] Is all feedback equally valued in digital spaces? Is this a version of ethical universalism? While scholars continue to debate these questions, it is clear that the digital space provides a modern, yet complicated space for Habermas's public sphere.[24]

So, who partakes in the construction process? Weilbe et al. argue that lobbying efforts by organizations traditionally hold the loudest voices in and most measurable impact on the policy development process.[25] Historically, organizations paid large sums of money for lobbying firms to represent their interests to policymakers. Lobbyists have dominated the policymaking process because of their proximity to decision makers; the depth of resources at their disposal; and the success of their techniques, adapted from years of experience.[26] As a result, lobbyists as extensions of organizations, are largely viewed as a dominant force in the policy development process, particularly on digital issues.[27]

However, a growing body of research suggests that digital technologies have greatly increased the ability of public stakeholders to participate in the policymaking process. Fung argues that digital spaces where the public can provide feedback to policymakers have improved the amount of public input in policymaking. For example, Congressional members' use of Facebook and Twitter provides users with an opportunity to give feedback on proposed policies, answer questions, provide personal experiences and perspectives, and leave messages of dissent when opposing actions. While some scholars question the quality of this feedback and its contributions to policy development, most agree that social media and digital spaces provide unprecedented access to policymakers and improved communication between policymakers and stakeholders.[28]

Tactics such as providing feedback to members of Congress on social media are part of policy feedback theory. Again, evolving from social constructivism, this theory argues that feedback is a critical part of the policy development process. Although there are many media for eliciting such feedback, digital technologies have a distinct advantage: their global reach. While previous forms of policy feedback include open forums and phone calls to members of Congress, digital platforms allow users and members of the public from around the globe to contribute to policy discussions. While issues of access remain a concern, digital technologies remove location-based barriers to public participation. For example, studies on environmental policy reform in Lithuania and Great Britain revealed that online feedback was provided from users around the world, not just citizens of each country.[29]

For some scholars, this cross-national feedback produces globalized policies that reflect international interests, not just constituent or citizen involvement. On global issues such as climate change or nuclear waste management, global input is valuable and reflects collaborative international efforts.[30,31] This has also increased the solicitation and reception of global feedback on digital issues, such as network neutrality.[32] However, some scholars criticize that this global communication can provide unequal access to the digital dialectic and larger influence in specific regions.[33]

Policy feedback, regardless of where it is solicited globally, is closely tied to theories of digital dialogic communication and the relational approach to public relations. Most scholarship on digital dialogic communication focuses on the relationship of the public to organizations, arguing that organizations benefit when responding and incorporating public feedback into communication and strategic decisions. Similar to organizational requests and use of feedback online, policymakers request and use public comments to build and shape policies. Digital dialogic theory promotes public feedback as a benefit for aware organizations or individuals who seek to incorporate public input into decisions. Digital dialogic communication stresses that public feedback and communication is critical to the success of policy decisions and a feature of strong organizational practices. As Taylor, Kent and White note, "dialogue is a tool for effective and mutually rewarding... communication."[34]

Some of the earliest scholarship conceptualizing digital dialogic communication appears in the late 1990s; however, the process and concept appeared in organizational and governmental practice long before then. Further, as digital technologies changed and grew over 40 years, digital dialogic communication simultaneously evolved, providing the public with further opportunities for feedback and co-construction of network neutrality policies.

Although this is not a historical book, this background information is necessary to later analyze how various forces have shaped the policy and its impact on dialogic communication. This chapter clarifies this rather complicated history by breaking down the history into sections and identifying four periods of network neutrality history. Each period is explained using a historical approach that outlines major developments as well as the forces impacting network neutrality. In addition, each time period provides a reflection on dialogic communication and public engagement with the concept at the time.

Period One: Internet's Wild West

Since the earliest iterations of the internet, individuals have sought to control the communication medium and apply various forms of policies to regulate public, organizational and governmental use. While the history of the internet dates back long before the 1980s, it was during this period that the first (minimal) regulatory policies began. These policies were primarily controlled by nonprofits and digital collectives or groups of individuals with interests in access and content. These groups grappled with issues of digital ownership and creating efficient and effective practices for intra-network communication. Goldsmith and Wu note that the earliest rules and policies on the internet emerged from trolling or attacking behaviors on "multiple user dungeons" (MUDs). Despite hopes that the internet would be a "new frontier, where people lived in peace, under their own rules, liberated from the constraints of an oppressive society and free from government meddling," the trolling behaviors clearly identified that some rules were necessary to prevent further problems.[35] LambdaMOO, one of the largest MUDs, became the first to form rules that would address problems of trolling.[36] Importantly, these rules were not handed down from the creators of the MUD but rather constructed through the text-based discussions of participants.[37] Mookin notes that the development of laws in LambdaMOO mirrors the development of other early internet policies in the 1980s and early 1990s. These policies were co-constructed by members of the MUD community rather than appointed or prescribed by individual leaders. Through these discussions, participants not only discursively constructed and labeled deviant behaviors but also constructed the nature of "digital community" for the first time.[38]

In this sense, the earliest internet rules and policies emerged directly from participants and members of MUD communities through dialogue. *Newsweek* summarized the ability of the community to identify and regulate itself as one of the greatest possibilities of the new digital world.[39] This type of early construction of digital policy is similar to digital dialogic practices, where the organization co-constructs rules and policies based on adjustments made from user or public feedback.

While there were no official representatives of LambdaMoo present in these policy discussions (because they did not have an individual who served in this official capacity), the act of co-construction and the use of community input align with the nature of dialogue. Years later, when organizations started to have an official presence on these sites, digital dialogic communication emerged as an adaptation of this earlier co-construction process. In short, the policy discussions in MUDs serve as the beginning of digital dialogic communication in the policy development process.

As policy and rule conversations continued to evolve in MUDs, advocacy groups, such as the Electronic Frontier Foundation (EFF), emerged as digital collectives of concerned users. Established in 1990, the group sought to develop "the legal conception of cyberspace as a separate place."[40] Bankston notes that the EFF served as a type of collective rather than as an organization with centralized leadership.[41] Similar to earlier discussions in MUDs, the EFF engaged its members in conversation over the direction and policy stance of the collective. Later, Morrison expressed the idea that EFF leader John Perry Barlow's vision for an internet devoid of governmental regulation was doomed from the start.[42] EFF sought to separate the internet from international government regulation and establish cyberspace as an independent region. Barlow wrote the "Declaration of Cyberspace Independence" as an email, and it later gained traction online to combat the "Communications Decency Act," created by the United States in 1996. Then, through a Supreme Court decision in 1997, parts of the Act that pertained to obscene material were overturned on First Amendment grounds. Thus, the first federal policy over internet content was struck down in what Barlow called a victory for digital independence. However, it should be noted that Section 230 of the Communications Decency Act provides immunity for online intermediaries for material published by a third party.[43] But this immunity has not prevented what some scholars refer to as a chilling effect or the suppression of free speech via the threat of legal action.[44,45]

Barlow's was not the only group to shape future policy discussions. Other nongovernmental individuals helped shape early network neutrality policies (or policies that predated neutrality) through academic and technological insight. Goldsmith and Wu identify "Larry Roberts, Robert Kahn, Vint Cerf, Jon Postel and Dave Clark" as individuals who helped design the digital structures that would later become network neutrality.[46] Specifically, they designed the internet as "neutral between applications," meaning that all internet uses (such as email, MUDs and downloads) were weighed the same and not prioritized based on pay or size. Although the group of founders and designers was not open to public comments or feedback, it formed a type of "working consensus" which was later compared to a type of early digital public sphere in its policy or rule formation process. While not an open community, such as those found in later discussions on network neutrality, the group did communicate and co-construct these policies throughout the early 1990s.[47] Here lies one of the challenges to Linklater's argument that the internet could provide equal voice for all participants (even those traditionally left out). While the group of policy builders did produce dialogue within their small community, it was not an open space and excluded many voices.

However, toward the end of this period, larger organizations bidding on government contracts began to take control of internet access and thus became more invested in impacting and controlling digital policies. Although it was previously users who gave feedback to impact internet policy and scope, organizations began using traditional lobbying efforts to shape issues of access, control and reach. By 1998, organizations such as Network Solutions financially bid for control of root authority (the connection services between users and a website) though the US Government. Although Jon Postel, an employee of the University of Southern California, traditionally maintained root authority and fought for control from the large corporation, eventually, Network Solutions won a contract from the Department of Defense that stripped him of his ability to regulate these connections. It was the end of individual and collective control over internet policies, and the beginning of organizational leadership.

Period Two: Regulatory Reform

The 1996 Telecommunications Act reflects organizational control over internet regulation and network neutrality policies.[48] Monumental lobbying efforts by American Telephone and Telegraph (AT&T) and Comcast during this time are considered largely responsible for the passage of the Act as well as other smaller policies that shifted network neutrality regulation. Kim et al. note that throughout the 1990s, large organizations gained more presence on the internet.[49] While most organizations started with individual websites, the growing number of digital message boards, early versions of third-party review sites and corporate emails encouraged competition for user engagement and attention. Growing digital competition meant that organizations needed to find creative ways to manage digital connection and presence. The success of large telecommunication organizations like

Network Solutions, who first vied for government contracts over root authority, inspired countless other telecommunication organizations to similarly attempt to control parts of cyberspace. Government contracts were not a viable possibility for all organizations seeking control and user access, but this did not prevent them from taking on lobbying initiatives. Lobbying became the primary mechanism for the quest for digital power and control over regulations during this period.

At stake for large telecommunication organizations was the ability to operate without government oversight and control. The 1996 Act promised to dramatically reduce the ability of the FCC to regulate corporate mergers and competition. Thus, as lawmakers drafted and proposed this legislation, large organizations sent lobbyists to Washington to advocate for corporate positioning. Derek Turner, founder of *Free Press,* wrote, "the powerful media and telecommunications giants and their army of overpaid lobbyists went straight to work obstructing and undermining the competition the new law was intended to create."[50] Organizations vied for policymaker attention and advocated for anti-competition clauses that would benefit the financial gains and opportunities of each company digitally.

The 1996 Act was largely considered an evolution of the earlier Communication Act of 1934, which established the FCC's responsibilities and control over the growing telecommunications activities in the United States.[51] The 1996 Act repealed and updated sections of the 1934 Act, specifically responding to the perception that the 1934 Act created monopolies, such as AT&T (because it stifled competition between telecommunication organizations). Specifically, the Act aimed "to provide for a pro-competitive, de-regulatory national policy framework designed to accelerate rapidly private sector deployment of advanced information technologies and services to all Americans by opening all telecommunications markets to competition."[52] Competition became a major focus of the 1996 Act, particularly as lawmakers sought opportunities to encourage digital competition, and this manifested within the two titles of the 1996 Act.

Under the second title, media can be classified as telecommunications or common carrier, thus requiring service providers to provide equal or neutral access to all content, regardless of size or paid relationship to an Internet Service Provider (ISP). Years later, in 2015, the FCC reclassified the internet as a telecommunications medium under Title II, thus formalizing a policy of network neutrality and giving the FCC the power to enforce such a policy.[53] Prior to the 2015 FCC decision, network neutrality was a voluntary principle of ISPs (which was often enforced through government oversight of merger agreements;

see Chapter 4 for more details). However, it was the policies created during the second period that laid the groundwork for network neutrality in the coming years.

Wright notes that while policymakers elicited no feedback from everyday users, feedback was consistently elicited from lobbyists and corporate representatives during this period.[54] In fact, although policymakers often boasted that the Act was incredibly popular with constituents, research demonstrates that most of the public opposed or was uninterested in the policy.[55] Atkin et al. note that the negative public reaction partially stagnated the implementation of the Acts provisions for the first ten years.[56] Findings from the Brookings Institute noted that although the 1996 Act claimed "public interest" at its core, there were few steps taken by policymakers to elicit or include public feedback.[57] Horwitz writes that "public interest" theories of regulation are the oldest types of theories used to discuss government regulation and that generally, public interest theory refers to a type of regulation that "is established in response to the conflict between private corporations and the general public."[58]

In their reflection on the first 20 years of the 1996 Act's implementation, Wright at al. argue that the little public feedback within the Act propelled later public dissatisfaction and perhaps encouraged public protest of and engagement in the issue around the early 2000s. For digital users who appreciated the co-constructionist era of early digital policy, the 1996 Act appeared as policy handed down from political elites.[59] And, although the policy now regulated much of digital access and content online (even if it was deregulatory policy), users were poised to retaliate and grapple for control over the continually evolving communication medium.[60]

Period Three: Wrestling for Control

The third period, beginning shortly after the new millennium, featured organizations and public representatives wrestling for control over network neutrality policies. The period witnessed a dramatic rise in online sites that sought to take power and control back from traditional large telecommunication organizations (or at least challenge its power). This included music file sharing sites such as BitTorrent, who later accused ISPs of blocking users attempting to access its website (a violation of network neutrality). In addition, a number of online sites facilitating dialogic communication premiered and grew popular, including third-party review sites (like Yelp), online networks for public engagement (like 4chan) and early social networks (like Friendster and MeetUp.org). The public turned to two-way communication facilitated through the internet to challenge organizational control at the same time that smaller organizations attempted to challenge larger telecommunications giants.

One of the earliest examples of the growing backlash against large telecommunication organizations' control over digital accessibility was a 2005 FCC order against ISP Madison River Communications. The ISP blocked user access to a competing Voice over IP (VoIP) phone service (i.e. internet phone calls).[61] The FCC argued that Madison River Communications slowed down and blocked access in order to promote its own VoIP services, outraging both competing VoIP companies as well as local users. In short, consumer demands for access to competition strained large telecommunication organizations and caused them to push back through legal channels. The FCC order set the stage for the 2005 Supreme Court "Brand X" decision just months later.

"Brand X" was a nondescript ISP with support from several large ISP petitioners who were concerned with the FCC's classification of the internet as an "information service." Large telecommunication organizations wanted to classify cable broadband as a telecommunications service that would be regulated based on the common carrier regulation of the 1996 Telecommunications Act. Earlier, the FCC argued that "all broadband services were presumptively subject to Title II common carrier regulation, including tariff, interconnection, and wholesale access requirements,"[62] meaning that the FCC could enforce a policy of network neutrality. The US Supreme Court agreed and ruled in favor of the FCC against Brand X, thus allowing the FCC to continue enforcing a policy of network neutrality.

Nunziato reflects that the "Brand X" case was motivated by growing frustrations from large telecommunication organizations, such as AT&T. In 2005, AT&T legally fought the City of Portland as it acquired local cable broadband service Telecommunications Inc (TCI). The city wanted to mandate open access of other ISPs as a condition of the acquisition, while AT&T did not want to be controlled by the same franchising provisions as other cable services. Its strained attempts to gain competitive advantages in Portland demonstrated larger battles over control of internet policy between the large telecommunication organizations, the FCC and the public.

Nunzianto adds the importance of this period:

> They herald a transition from an Internet governed by a nondiscriminatory principle facilitating the free flow of information to an Internet that is subject to discrimination and bottleneck control

by a small handful of network operators... Given the current regulatory regime, we now find ourselves in a state in which expression in cyberspace is subject to the dictates of the private entities who serve as gatekeepers for Internet expression, and those private entities are not subject to any meaningful constraints on their ability to discriminate against expression.[63]

So, how did this period of wrestling for control turn into a period of dramatic shifts in network neutrality policy? Howard contends that public involvement and popular pressure were largely responsible for this shift and simultaneously reflect the current period in regulation.[64]

Period Four: Engagement and Impact

The fourth and current period reflects the lasting legacy of engagement and impact foreshadowed during the third period. It should also be noted that as "digital engagement and advocacy increased in availability and popularity with the public, various governments also began to be able to respond in open and transparent ways, as well as with misinformation and surveillance tactics."[65] As digital spaces for feedback and two-way communication continued to proliferate, public perspective was elicited and incorporated into digital policies on network neutrality. The 2015 decision to uphold network neutrality was framed as a direct reflection of public advocacy. Howard reflects, "aside from being a solution to recurring legal difficulties, it was a response to popular pressure."[66] FCC Chairperson Tom Wheeler added,

> We heard from startups and world-leading tech companies. We heard from ISPs, large and small. We heard from public-interest groups and public-policy think tanks. We heard from Members of Congress, and yes, the President. Most importantly, we heard from nearly 4 million Americans who overwhelming spoke up in favor of preserving a free and open Internet.[67]

The remainder of this book examines how these four million voices were cultivated against the backdrop of changes to network neutrality policy.

Wheeler's quote summarizes the fourth period nearly perfectly: the myriad of voices and positions constructing public policy using two-way communication. Nearly all of Wheeler's participating parties used two-way communication to engage the public and co-construct policy developments. First, the FCC requested feedback on its public commenting system. Second, organizations such as Reddit asked users to call Congressional representatives in support of network neutrality policies. Third, media personalities and journalists, such as John Oliver, requested that audience members give feedback to the FCC. Digital two-way communication became the mechanism for this engagement in the months before the 2015 FCC decision in favor of network neutrality policies.

However, the period of organizational and lobbying input was not over. Just two years later, the FCC voted to repeal network neutrality, a decision which many claimed was a result of organizational lobbying efforts. OpenSecrets.org, the online political watchdog monitoring lobbying efforts, reported that nearly 100 quarterly lobbying reports from those who lobby the FCC mentioned network neutrality during 2017.[68] These lobbying groups represented 18 telecommunication organizations who wanted to eliminate network neutrality policies, spending nearly $110 million over the course of the year. ISP Comcast Corporation spent nearly $4 million lobbying Congress on network neutrality from 2016 to 2017. The results, according to *Medium*, were the swift repeal of network neutrality in 2017, despite millions of public posts of support on the FCC's public commenting website.[69] *Fortune* reflected that the 2015 and 2017 decisions ignited passion on both sides of the debate.[70] On the one hand, the 2015 verdict reflected the successful impact of public engagement and evidence of a dialogue between the FCC and stakeholders; on the other hand, the 2017 repeal reflected the continued success of organizational lobbying efforts.

This tension between dialogic practices and organizational lobbying efforts is viewed globally as countries such as India and Great Britain also seek the means to shape and create network neutrality policies. For example, while the United Kingdom has traditionally operated using the European Union's (EU's) network neutrality rules, the 2017 Brexit decision (for the United Kingdom to leave the EU) could possibly change the United Kingdom's enforcement of network neutrality.[71] The United Kingdom's Channel 4 News reflected, "People on both sides of the debate will no doubt try putting pressure on politicians."[72]

Similarly, after viewing the success of John Oliver's *Last Week Tonight* segment on network neutrality in 2014, proponents of network neutrality adopted a similar approach to galvanize support for the policy in India. The BBC reported that it was public pressure in India that spurred on some of the toughest network neutrality regulations in the world as massive protests and public campaigns encouraged policy leadership to design and enforce the digital policy.[73] Publications such as *USA Today* were quick to juxtapose the actions on network neutrality taken in India with those taken in the United States during 2017.[74] While Indian regulators incorporated public feedback and digital dialogic communication in their actions, the United States favored lobbying efforts and ignored public advocacy.[75]

The oscillation between public and organizational engagement and power in the network neutrality debate hallmarks the fourth period. The remainder of this book examines how governmental, organizational, media, public and advocacy groups have enacted this engagement and impact within the contemporary network neutrality debate.

Dialogic Communication and Network Neutrality

As each period demonstrates, there are instances of various stakeholders taking control of the internet and network neutrality. In addition, stakeholders debate and jockey for control throughout each period using digital communication. This is evidenced by the overload of the 2015 FCC commenting system, where millions of comments were registered, crashing the site. Or, during the development of the 1996 Telecommunications Act, where organizational lobbyists engaged members of Congress and regulators to shape policy in favorable ways. In short, two-way communication has proliferated throughout the evolution of the internet and network neutrality.

However, network neutrality policies were not just shaped by communication; the policy also holds the ability to facilitate or prevent dialogic exchanges from taking place at all. Shell reflects that a repeal of network neutrality would give ISPs the ability to determine access between organizations and the public, thus challenging free speech and the open sharing of ideas in a digital space.[76] For example, an ISP can reduce access to sites that present political views that counter or challenge the ISP's.[77] This could include news outlets, advocacy groups and even social platforms where dialogues take place. Sommerfelt, Kent and Taylor argue that these advocacy groups should be the key to upholding digital dialogic communication because they provide organizations with feedback and insight into public opinion.[78] If access to public advocacy groups is de-prioritized or limited, digital dialogic communication is stifled. Policies of network neutrality are necessary to realize the full potential of digital dialogic communication.[79]

The next few chapters illustrate how dialogic communication impacts the network neutrality debate from the perspective of key stakeholders. This includes government, regulatory, journalistic, organizational, public and global perspectives. While network neutrality policy continues to emerge and change (beyond the four periods), dialogic communication stands to shape and be shaped by network neutrality. The fourth period, marked by the swing of control between public and organizational interests, is illuminated and explained through these perspectives, allowing for predictions over future regulatory trends.

Notes

1 Felix Simon, "Why No One Seems to Care about Net Neutrality." *Medium,* December 10, 2017. https://medium.com/@FelixSimon/why-no-one-seems-to-care-about-net-neutrality-b4b7fb9f85a8.
2 Nina Eliasoph, *"Do It Yourself Democracy: The Rise of the Public Engagement Industry."* by Caroline W. Lee. New York: Oxford University Press, 2015: 292.
3 Christopher M. Weible, Paul A. Sabatier, and Kelly McQueen, "Themes and Variations: Taking Stock of the Advocacy Coalition Framework." *Policy Studies Journal* 37, no. 1 (2009): 121–140.
4 Christopher M. Weible, Tanya Heikkila, Peter deLeon, and Paul A. Sabatier, "Understanding and Influencing the Policy Process." *Policy Sciences* 45, no. 1 (2012): 1–21. doi:10.1007/s11077-011-9143-5.
5 Jan Meyers and Martha MacDonald, "Reciprocal Relationships: The Role of Government and the Social Economy in the Co-Construction of Social Policy in Atlantic Canada." *Canadian Public Policy/Analyse De Politiques* 40, no. Supplement 1 (2014): S17–S25.
6 Troels Fage Hedegaard, "The Policy Design Effect: Proximity as a Micro-Level Explanation of the Effect of Policy Designs on Social Benefit Attitudes." *Scandinavian Political Studies* 37, no. 4 (2014): 366–384.
7 Jenny Andersson and Anne-Greet Keizer, "Governing the Future: Science, Policy and Public Participation in the Construction of the Long Term in the Netherlands and Sweden." *History and Technology* 30, no. 1–2 (2014): 104–122.
8 Ching Ching Leong, Darryl Jarvis, Michael Howlett, and Andrea Migone, "Controversial Science-Based Technology Public Attitude Formation and Regulation in Comparative Perspective: The State Construction of Policy Alternatives in Asia." *Technology in Society* 33, no. 1 (2011): 128–136.
9 Anne Schneider and Mara Sidney, "What Is Next for Policy Design and Social Construction Theory?" *Policy Studies Journal* 37, no. 1 (2009): 103.
10 Jonathan J. Pierce, Saba Siddiki, Michael D. Jones, Kristin Schumacher, Andrew Pattison, and Holly Peterson, "Social Construction and Policy Design: A Review of Past Applications." *Policy Studies Journal* 42, no. 1 (2014): 1–29.
11 Nicholeen DeGrasse-Johnson, *Towards the Construction of a National Dance Education Policy in Jamaica: Public Education Curriculum and Ownership.* Archived Dissertation, Temple University, 2014.
12 Jonathan J. Pierce, Saba Siddiki, Michael D. Jones, Kristin Schumacher, Andrew Pattison, and Holly Peterson, "Social Construction and Policy Design: A Review of Past Applications." *Policy Studies Journal* 42, no. 1 (2014): 1–29.
13 Paul Pierson, "When Effect Becomes Cause: Policy Feedback and Political Change." *World Politics* 45, no. 4 (1993): 595–628.

14 Sarah Elwood and Katharyne Mitchell, "Mapping Children's Politics: Spatial Stories, Dialogic Relations and Political Formation." *Geografiska Annaler: Series B, Human Geography* 94, no. 1 (2012): 1–15.

15 Ibid., p. 1.

16 Michael L. Kent and Maureen Taylor, "Toward a Dialogic Theory of Public Relations." *Public Relations Review* 28, no. 1 (2002): 21–37.

17 Maureen Taylor and Michael L. Kent, "Dialogic Engagement: Clarifying Foundational Concepts." *Journal of Public Relations Research* 26, no. 5 (2014): 384–398.

18 Andrew Linklater, "Dialogic Politics and the Civilising Process." *Review of International Studies* 31, no. 1 (2005): 141–154.

19 Robert Wapshott and Oliver Mallett, "The Unspoken Side of Mutual Adjustment: Understanding Intersubjective Negotiation in Small Professional Service Firms." *International Small Business Journal* 31, no. 8 (2013): 978–996.

20 Jim Macnamara, "Organizational Listening: Addressing a Major Gap in Public Relations Theory and Practice." *Journal of Public Relations Research* 28, no. 3–4 (2016): 146–169.

21 Petra Theunissen and Wan Norbani Wan Noordin, "Revisiting the Concept 'Dialogue' in Public Relations." *Public Relations Review* 38, no. 1 (2012): 5.

22 Michael Paquette, Erich J. Sommerfeldt, and Michael L. Kent, "Do the Ends Justify the Means? Dialogue, Development Communication, and Deontological Ethics." *Public Relations Review* 41, no. 1 (2015): 30–39.

23 Andrew Linklater, "Dialogic Politics and the Civilising Process." *Review of International Studies* 31, no. 1 (2005): 141–154.

24 Alexander Jenkins, Alexander Nikolaev, and Douglas V. Porpora, "Moral Reasoning and the Online Debate about Iraq." *Political Communication* 29, no. 1 (2012): 44–63.

25 Christopher M. Weible, Paul A. Sabatier, and Kelly McQueen, "Themes and Variations: Taking Stock of the Advocacy Coalition Framework." *Policy Studies Journal* 37, no. 1 (2009): 121–140.

26 Wesley J. Leckrone and Justin Gollob, "The Effectiveness of Intergovernmental Lobbying Mechanisms in the American Federal System." *Fédéralisme Régionalisme* 12 (2012).

27 Anthony J. Nownes, *Total Lobbying: What Lobbyists Want (and How They Try to Get It)*. Cambridge; New York: Cambridge University Press, 2006.

28 Frank R. Baumgartner, *Lobbying and Policy Change: Who Wins, Who Loses, and Why*. Chicago: University of Chicago Press, 2009.

29 Luka Vavtar, "Environmental Lobby Effectiveness – The Case of Lithuania and the United Kingdom." *Socialinių Mokslų Studijos* 6, no. VI/2 (2014): 313–330.

30 Andrew Jordan and Elah Matt, "Designing Policies that Intentionally Stick: Policy Feedback in a Changing Climate." *Policy Sciences* 47, no. 3 (2014): 227–247.

31 Matthew C. Nowlin, "Policy Change, Policy Feedback, and Interest Mobilization: The Politics of Nuclear Waste Management." *Review of Policy Research* 33, no. 1 (2016): 51–70.

32 Christine M. Stover, "Network Neutrality: A Thematic Analysis of Policy Perspectives across the Globe." *Global Media Journal* 3, no. 1 (2010): 75.

33 David J. Yates, Girish J. Gulati, and Anas Tawileh, "Explaining the Global Digital Divide: The Impact of Public Policy Initiatives on Digital Opportunity and ICT Development." 2010. doi:10.1109/HICSS.2010.196.

34 Maureen Taylor, Michael L. Kent, and William J. White, "How Activist Organizations Are Using the Internet to Build Relationships." *Public Relations Review* 27, no. 3 (2001): 267.

35 Jack L. Goldsmith and Tim Wu, *Who Controls the Internet? Illusions of a Borderless World.* New York: Oxford University Press, 2006: 13.

36 Diane J. Schiano, "Lessons from LambdaMOO: A Social, Text-Based Virtual Environment." *Presence: Teleoperators & Virtual Environments* 8, no. 2 (1999): 127–139.

37 Jennifer L. Mnookin, "Virtual(Ly) Law: The Emergence of Law in LambdaMOO: Mnookin." *Journal of Computer-Mediated Communication* 2, no. 1 (1996).

38 Lecia Jane Barker, "'Real People, Real Interaction – Even onnaMOO': The Discursive Construction of Virtual Community on LambdaMOO." ProQuest Dissertations Publishing, 1998.

39 Katie Hafner, *Get in the MOOd. (LambdaMOO, a Multi-User Dungeon on the Internet).* Vol. 124. New York: Newsweek LLC, 1994.

40 Jack L. Goldsmith and Tim Wu, *Who Controls the Internet? Illusions of a Borderless World.* New York: Oxford University Press, 2006: 18.

41 Kevin Bankston, "A Tale of Two Dystopias: Order and Chaos on the Electronic Frontier." *American Journal of Criminal Law* 43, no. 2 (2016): 157.

42 Aimée Hope Morrison, "An Impossible Future: John Perry Barlow's 'Declaration of the Independence of Cyberspace'." *New Media & Society* 11, no. 1–2 (2009): 53–71.

43 Urs Gasser and Wolfgang Schulz, "Governance of Online Intermediaries: Observations from a Series of National Case Studies." *SSRN Electronic Journal* 7641, (2015): 1–283.

44 Siva Vaidhyanathan, "Critical Information Studies: A Bibliographic Manifesto." *SSRN Electronic Journal*, no. 1 (2005): 1–36. doi:10.2139/ssrn.788984.

45 Jonathon W. Penney, "Internet Surveillance, Regulation, and Chilling Effects Online: A Comparative Case Study." *Internet Policy Review* 6, no. 2 (2017): 1–37. doi:10.14763/2017.2.692.

46 Jack L. Goldsmith and Tim Wu, *Who Controls the Internet? Illusions of a Borderless World.* New York: Oxford University Press, 2006: 20.

47 Mariarosaria Taddeo, "The Struggle between Liberties and Authorities in the Information Age." *Science and Engineering Ethics* 21, no. 5 (2015): 1125–1138.

48 Justin S. Brown, "Revisiting the Telecommunications Act of 1996." *PS, Political Science & Politics* 51, no. 1 (2018): 129.

49 Minjeong Kim, Jang Hyun Kim, and Chung Joo Chung, "Who Shapes Network Neutrality Policy Debate? An Examination of Information Subsidizers in the Mainstream Media and at Congressional and FCC Hearings." *Telecommunications Policy* 35, no. 4 (2011): 314–324.

50 S. Derek Turner, "Dismantling Digital Deregulation." Free Press (2018). www.freepress.net/sites/default/files/fp-legacy/Dismantling_Digital_Deregulation.pdf.

51 FCC, "Telecommunications Act of 1996." www.fcc.gov/general/tele
    communications-act-1996.
52 Conference Report, Telecommunications Act of 1996, House of Repre-
    sentatives, 104th Congress, 2d Session, H.Rept. 104–458, at p. 1.
53 Fran Berkman and Andrew Couts, "Title II Is the Key to Net Neutrality,
    So What Is It?" *DailyDot*, May 20, 2014. www.dailydot.com/layer8/
    what-is-title-ii-net-neutrality-fcc/.
54 Christopher J. Wright, Rick Boucher, James L. Casserly, Jim Cicconi,
    Charles M. Davidson, Michele Farquhar, and George S. Ford et al.,
    "Reflecting on Twenty Years under the Telecommunications Act of 1996:
    A Collection of Essays on Implementation." *Federal Communications Law
    Journal* 68, no. 1 (2015): 44.
55 Reed E. Hundt, "Ten Years under the 1996 Telecommunications Act."
    Federal Communications Law Journal 58, no. 3 (2006): 399.
56 David J. Atkin, Tuen-Yu Lau, and Carolyn A. Lin, "Still on Hold? A Ret-
    rospective Analysis of Competitive Implications of the Telecommunication
    Act of 1996, on Its 10th Year Anniversary." *Telecommunications Policy* 30,
    no. 2 (2006): 80–95.
57 Stuart N. Brotman, "Revisiting the Broadcast Public Standard in Com-
    munications Law and Regulation." *Brookings Institute*, March 23, 2017.
    www.brookings.edu/research/revisiting-the-broadcast-public-interest-
    standard-in-communications-law-and-regulation/.
58 Robert Britt Horwitz, *The Irony of Regulatory Reform: The Deregulation
    of American Telecommunications.* New York: Oxford University Press.
59 Patricia Aufderheide, "Shifting Policy Paradigms and the Public Interest
    in the U.S. Telecommunications Act of 1996." *The Communication Review*
    2, no. 2 (1997): 259–281.
60 Thomas W. Hazlett, "Economic and Political Consequences of the 1996
    Telecommunications Act." *Regulation* 23, no. 3 (2000): 36.
61 FCC, "Order: Madison River Communications." March 3, 2005. https://
    apps.fcc.gov/edocs_public/attachmatch/DA-05-543A1.pdf.
62 Wiley Rein, "Summary of the Supreme Court's Decision in *National
    Cable & Telecommunications Association v. Brand X Internet Services and
    FCC v. Brand X Internet Services.*" June 27, 2005. www.wileyrein.com/
    newsroom-pressreleases-161.html.
63 Dawn C. Nunziato, *Virtual Freedom: Net Neutrality and Free Speech in the
    Internet Age.* California: Stanford Law Books, 2007: 127.
64 Matthew Howard, *Net Neutrality for Broadband: Understanding the FCC's
    2015 Open Internet Order.* New York: Puma Concolor Aeternus Press,
    2015: 15.
65 Zeynep Tufekci, *Twitter and Tear Gas: The Power and Fragility of
    Networked Protest.* New Haven: Yale University Press, 2017.
66 Matthew Howard, *Net Neutrality for Broadband: Understanding the FCC's
    2015 Open Internet Order.* New York: Puma Concolor Aeternus Press,
    2015: 15.
67 Ibid., p. 15.
68 Geoff West, "Money Flows into Net Neutrality Debate ahead of
    FCC Vote." *Open Secrets*, December 14, 2017. www.opensecrets.org/
    news/2017/12/money-flows-into-net-neutrality-debate-ahead-of-fcc-vote/.

69 Andrew Jerell Jones, "Comcast Spends Millions in Lobbying on Net Neutrality without Their News Networks Disclosing Their Spending." *Medium*, July 10, 2017. https://medium.com/theyoungturks/comcast-spends-millions-in-lobbying-on-net-neutrality-without-their-news-networks-disclosing-their-499b3d9cb6dd.

70 Aaron Pressman, "Net Neutrality Repeal Stirs Passion on Each Side." *Fortune*, December 14, 2017. http://fortune.com/2017/12/14/net-neutrality-verizon-neflix-comcast/.

71 Andrew Griffin, "Net Neutrality Repeal in the US Could Threaten Internet Freedom in the UK, Warn Campaigners." *The Independent*, December 15, 2017. www.independent.co.uk/life-style/gadgets-and-tech/news/net-neutrality-repeal-vote-results-us-uk-fcc-internet-freedom-europe-a8113076.html.

72 Martin Williams, "Net neutrality: Should We Be Worried." *Channel 4 News*, November 28, 2017. www.channel4.com/news/factcheck/net-neutrality-should-we-be-worried.

73 Prasanto K. Roy, "India Net Neutrality Rules Could Be World's Strongest." *BBC News*, November 30, 2017. www.bbc.com/news/world-asia-india-42162979.

74 Mike Snider and Elizabeth Weise, "John Oliver May Have Helped Spur 15000 Comments to FCC on Net Neutrality." *USA Today*, May 9, 2017. www.usatoday.com/story/tech/talkingtech/2017/05/09/john-oliver-may-have-helped-spur-150000-comments-fcc-net-neutrality/101480100/.

75 FE Online, "India Upholds Net Neutrality but Here Is John Oliver's Take on America's Woes." *Financial Express*, December 13, 2017. www.financialexpress.com/india-news/india-upholds-net-neutrality-but-here-is-john-olivers-hilarious-take-on-americas-woes/972610/.

76 Meredith Shell, "Network Neutrality and Broadband Service Providers' First Amendment Right to Free Speech." *Federal Communications Law Journal* 66, no. 2 (2014): 303.

77 Marvin Ammori, "Beyond Content Neutrality: Understanding Content-Based Promotion of Democratic Speech." *Federal Communications Law Journal* 61, no. 2 (2009): 273.

78 Erich J. Sommerfeldt, Michael L. Kent, and Maureen Taylor, "Activist Practitioner Perspectives of Website Public Relations: Why Aren't Activist Websites Fulfilling the Dialogic Promise?" *Public Relations Review* 38, no. 2 (2012): 303.

79 Maureen Taylor, Michael L. Kent, and William J. White, "How Activist Organizations Are Using the Internet to Build Relationships." *Public Relations Review* 27, no. 3 (2001): 263–284.

2 Political and Governmental Interpretations

On December 14, 2017, the Federal Communications Commission (FCC) voted to eliminate the 2015 order of network neutrality, led by Chairman Ajit Pai. Although many foresaw this outcome, particularly because of Pai's outspoken commentary promising to eliminate the policy, journalists scrambled to predict what would happen next.[1] Considering the widespread public support for network neutrality, how would public, advocacy groups and elected officials respond? As organizations, advocates and members of the public from around the world released official and unofficial responses on social media, media interviews and websites, Congressman Bob Doyle (D-PA) released an official statement condemning the decision and advocating for Congressional intervention to prevent the FCC's policy from actualizing:

> I've tried repeatedly to convince Chairman Pai to abandon his plans to dismantle the Open Internet Order – most recently by organizing a letter from 118 Members of Congress urging him not to take this vote today – and now that the FCC has voted to kill Net Neutrality and give ISPs a green light to control access to the Internet, I will introduce legislation under the Congressional Review Act to overturn today's order and restore Net Neutrality.[2]

Doyle, along with ten other representatives, openly condemned the reversal of policy, and promised quick Congressional action to overturn the FCC's ruling.

Congressman Doyle remained the face of Congressional action in the following months, providing updates through press conferences, digital media and his official House website.[3] In particular, Doyle's website provided visual interpretations of network neutrality and answers to frequently asked questions alongside bolded contact information to share public concerns and questions about the policy.[4] Doyle's legislation to overturn the FCC's ruling gained momentum and within a month, he gained an additional 30 cosponsors (bringing his total to 110). Although he had enough support to bring his legislation to the Congressional floor for comment, he needed to wait for the FCC to officially submit its policy to Congress for review. While he waited, Doyle maintained public engagement through a variety of media formats, even holding daily press briefings.[5]

Key to Doyle's success was finding bipartisan support for his proposed legislation. While Doyle, a Democrat, elicited support from his fellow Democratic representatives, he failed to obtain any support or cosponsors from Republican or Independent backgrounds.[6] Similar legislation within the Senate, proposed by Senator Ed Markey (D-MA), only obtained one Republican cosponsor, meaning it was short one additional Republican for the 51-vote majority needed.[7] *The Atlantic* reflected that the political leanings of support for the House and Senate proposals demonstrated that network neutrality had become a key political issue.[8]

Powell and Cooper showed that network neutrality had successfully transformed from solely a technology issue to one that was distinctly "political," particularly in the United States.[9] Discursive creation and rendering through advocacy (since Tim Wu's 2003 article) had the desired effect in the public conscious in taking a very complex technical issue and discursively rendering it politically relevant to partisan politics and the public consciousness.

Discourses are important as they reflect the positions of political leaders as they fight, debate and consider the FCC's role in regulating network neutrality. Through an analysis of political mentions of network neutrality, this chapter identifies the four discourses that politicians used to describe the issue. Previous scholarship identified political discourses as important because of its adoption by media and public. In addition, discourses are a way to examine the decision-making process and context of political (or FCC) rulings.

Politicians, particularly political representatives, are critical to decisions about network neutrality. Although the FCC is the governing body that regulates the digital communication medium, Congress maintains the ability to overturn recently enacted legislation through the Congressional Review Act.[10] This means that through a Senate vote, the FCC's "Restoring Internet Freedom" proposal may be challenged and even rejected. Thus, political reflections on network neutrality from Congressional representatives are key to understanding the future of the policy.

Clark argues that network neutrality means different things to different stakeholders.[11] Part of the difficulty with the issue is the struggle to define and concretely identify the practices, policies and effects of the concept and its regulation. For liberal internet advocates, network neutrality debates are over the concept of a "free and open" digital space, where all content has an equal chance of being found by users.[12] For large multinational corporations, network neutrality means securing a revenue stream through increasing competition based on financial markets. Beyond these two engaged groups in the ongoing debate, other research suggests that the public, although one of the most impacted groups by a network neutrality ruling, conceptualizes the issue as "boring," "irrelevant" and "unimportant."[13] These conflicting definitions present a unique challenge for regulators attempting to create policies for the issue, journalists attempting to cover the debate and legislators who must balance the demands of public interest and corporate lobbying.

Ultimately, Cheng et al. conclude that network neutrality, at its core, is a debate over the purpose and economic constraints of the internet.[14] Traditionally, large corporations like Comcast oppose network neutrality and have advocated for a closed-internet system where corporations could bid and make financial arrangements for priority service from internet providers.[15] This would potentially prioritize larger companies who can afford to out-bit or out-price smaller entities. Alternatively, proponents of network neutrality support government regulation, through the FCC, where search and internet providers must give all digital content equal chances of being found.[16]

Verma notes that network neutrality is unique in its political position because it is not really a "party-based debate."[17] Instead, proponents and opponents (as well as neutral leaders) come from liberal and conservative backgrounds. While this may be a refreshing take on bipartisanship, other scholars argue that this lack of political allegiance to either side of the debate may be part of the difficulty of recruiting public support or dissent on the issue.[18] However, even with public support growing in the recent years, the issue remains "shrouded in an invisibility cloak from the public."[19]

It is the lack of information and opinions from the public on the issue of network neutrality that makes studying governmental representation so important. Scholars note that corporations and the media simultaneously silenced the debate and issue, and insulated it from the public.[20] Large telecommunication corporations might rather the public remain uninvolved in the issue, considering that their participation may encourage politicians and federal regulators to support network neutrality. Further, the media conclude that network neutrality is a "non-starter," an issue that is difficult to garner public interest due to its highly technical nature.[21] Thus, the issue is rarely discussed publicly by corporations or the media, which raises the barrier to discursive entry by the public. Kim et al. found that the only group willing to and readily discussing the issue in-view of the general public were politicians, federal regulators and other members of the federal government.[22] These individuals, in turn, greatly shaped the discourses of network neutrality for members of the public, particularly because of the absence of other views. Therefore, to examine what information is given to the public, researchers can look at these sources of network neutrality-themed discourses.

Scholarship that examines how the public forms opinions on complex policy initiatives and changes has identified two major sources of information and persuasion: the media and politicians. As mentioned previously, traditional media (i.e. newspapers) tended to stay away from the topic of network neutrality because of its difficulty to maintain audience interest in the topic.[23] Alternatively, politicians spoke frequently on the topic throughout its 30-year history in a variety of environments, including Congressional speeches, public forums, roundtables and political debates.[24] Although not widely attended or even viewed, these addresses sometimes serve as the only source of information on the topic for the general public. This is critical, as previous research identified that the public relies heavily on political discourses for information policy, especially when the issue is perceived as complex, irrelevant to their daily life, or unfamiliar.[25] Without competing or alternative media discourses, the messages and information presented in these political channels are often the building blocks of public opinion.[26]

Robinson found that the public often adopts the discourses presented in political communication, particularly on technical issues.[27] Without having their own experiences with the issue, the public will take on the positions, frames and discourses found within political speeches, addresses or debates.[28] Technical language, in particular, is frequently adopted first because of its close-ties to the specific issue; when the public uses the language, they feel as if they understand or know the issue.[29] On a complex technical issue like network neutrality, the discourses and language of politicians are centrally important to how the public perceives and then supports or opposes the issue.

Further research demonstrates that discourses from politicians are then frequently adopted by other news broadcasts, which further disseminates the message.[30] Political discourses of technical and media-related issues are also important to understanding the future of the media industry. Wu notes that the political debates over media regulations tend to reproduce themselves in a cyclical style throughout American history.[31] The debates over control of radio airwaves during the 1920s and 1930s look strikingly similar to the debates over control of television in the 1950s, phones in the 1980s and the internet in the 1990s.[32] Identifying the discourses surrounding network neutrality may give insight into future media issues including: spectrum auctions, network design and monopoly-busting activities.[33] Wu writes that the Telecommunication Act of 1996 shouldn't have surprised anyone; all you had to do was look at the political discourses of radio regulation in the 1930s to predict how politicians would frame the issue 60 years later.[34] In short, looking at the discourses of network neutrality today could give insight into the issue (and other issues) of the future.

Part of the difficulty with identifying politician discourses is the lack of centrality and consistency of political appearances. For example, members of Congress speak about network neutrality on the Congressional floor, at election campaign stops, during interviews, in roundtable debates and discussions, and in town hall meetings with constituents. This environmental diversity complicates researchers' ability to collect a comprehensive set of data regarding political speeches. While previous work has used the Congressional Record to examine how politicians frame political issues, the Congressional Record only covers speeches made on the Congressional floor. Further, members of Congress can strike comments, passages and entire speeches from the Record, meaning important data may be lost. Other research has used the personal campaign websites of politicians to watch or read speeches. However, these sites are carefully crafted and edited, meaning researchers may not get to see unedited footage or content.

In an effort to find an exhaustive source of data that includes the many environments of political speeches, this project uses the C-SPAN (Cable-Satellite Public Affairs Network) digital archives. The archives include transcripts and videos of all Congressional activities, including those mentioned earlier. Further, members of Congress do not have the ability to edit or modify the archives, so the data remains free of manipulation. Importantly, the archives include all recorded data, including those that are not shown on television. Media readily ignored the issue for most of its history, so the archives include political speeches that would have been left out of traditional media coverage. Other scholars estimate that the archives are roughly 95% complete, meaning they house and include the vast majority of politician (Congressional and Executive) activities, speeches and discourses. As a result, they make a strong dataset, considering the completeness and scope of their collection.

Emblematic of Our Time

First, politicians often engaged in reflexivity on network neutrality, which allows them to reflect on the importance of the topic and its relevance to contemporary American politics. Rather than providing a concrete definition of the topic, members of Congress spent time describing its place and pan-applicability as an issue. For example, consider former FCC Chair Michael Powell's (2014) reflection that network neutrality is a "great" issue of our time. Throughout Powell's 45-minute interview, the former Chair never defined network neutrality, nor did he come out in favor or against it. Instead, he discussed its application to other topics, such as internet searches, growing corporate competition and American leadership in digital policy.

This allusive type of discussion of network neutrality was common throughout political reflections. Often, politicians shied away from providing a concrete definition of the issue, but rather discussed its importance. Previous research suggests that this might be a reflection of the complexity of the issue, rather than a strategic decision. There are, as described earlier, many definitions of the term; thus, selecting one definition or one description may be a complicated choice for political leaders. Chip Pickering, the CEO of Comptel, and an invited Congressional speaker for the FCC, added his own difficulty with defining the term. Pickering tells members of Congress that the term is so complicated that even he cannot tell them what it means. Instead, he spends his five-minute speech on the ongoing importance of the issue, and its implications for the technology industry.

Other speakers were more specific with their analysis of the implications of network neutrality. During a meeting of the Committee on the Judiciary in 2013, Senator Blumenthal (D-CT) reflected that the definition of network neutrality was less important than the rules. He notes that network neutrality is a focus on rules and regulations. Again, this focus is on the implications rather than a direct analysis or description of the issue.

The focus on implications is an important part of the way politicians speak about network neutrality. Throughout the dataset, there were few cases where definitions were provided. Instead, this reflexivity, where politicians talk about implications but not identity, is present and dominant throughout. There are also other ways that political leaders discussed the network neutrality issue without providing a definition. Many reflected that the politicized nature of the topic was emblematic of our current political divide between Republicans and Democrats. Several speakers used the division over network neutrality to talk about the inability for either side to compromise, thus resulting in issue-standoffs and missing consensus. Congresswoman Marsha Blackburn (R-TN) noted in a 2005 speech on the future of technology, warned fellow members of Congress that issues such as network neutrality would be long battles over the frontier of digital technology due to the lack of compromise in Congress. Other speeches similarly discussed the political implications of network neutrality, using it as a case study for contentious politics.

Necessary for National Security

Three years later, Congresswoman Blackburn returned to speak about the frequency of cybersecurity attacks and the possible decline of national security. In her speech, she implored Congress to take digital issues, like network neutrality, firewalls and cyberterrorism seriously, and put aside the political divides that block progress. Like Blackburn's earlier speeches, she connects the issue of network neutrality to the political standoff that existed(s) between members of Congress from opposing political parties. However, it is her link to national security that is perhaps more representative of the second discourse. Frequently, network neutrality was linked to issues of national security, particularly cyberattacks and cyberterrorism. Although on its face, network neutrality has more to do with search engine operations than hacking culture, discursively, politicians remarked that inaction on network neutrality was remarkably similar to inaction on cybersecurity measures. In effect, network neutrality was a metaphor for political uncertainty and an inability to reconcile differences on technology-centered issues. Politicians such as Vice President Joe Biden, Senator Marco Rubio (R-FL) and Governor Chris Christie (R-NJ) all spoke out about the lack of compromises existing in federal government (particularly Congress) as potentially catastrophic for our cybersecurity. Comments like Rubio's, where network neutrality was emblematic of other digital issues, were common, especially as politicians spoke in front of Congress.

This type of speech is a type of meta-talk about network neutrality. Importantly, most politicians are not proposing legislation on the issue, or even providing solutions or their own position. Instead, they are talking about (and criticizing) inaction. This discourse is less about the issue, and more about the political stalemate. An interesting feature of this type of discourse was its prevalence among members of Congress. These speakers were critical of their fellow Congressmen, but didn't seem to propose any action to solve the problem. These speeches were mostly rhetorical, designed to distance the speaker from the action (or inaction) of Congress.

While more research would be necessary, it is possible that network neutrality was implicated in these discussions because of its familiarity with Congress. The jargon-heavy terminology of cybersecurity and hacking was less understandable than network neutrality, thus possibly serving as an easier example of these digital stalemates in Congress.

Corporate Presence

Throughout the 20 years of political discourse, speakers reflected on the ongoing presence of corporate interests in contemporary US policy. Many companies were implicated in these speeches; however, easily the most common were Comcast and Google. Throughout the dataset, Comcast was included in 549 speeches, roughly 18% of all speeches included in this analysis. Over the 20 years, descriptions of Comcast's stake in network neutrality varied, particularly as the company grew. The earliest mentions of Comcast (in 1996) reflect on how new digital technologies may help companies profit in a digital space. However, as time went on, speakers grew wary of Comcast's growing presence in the digital space, particularly as the company pressured political leaders and the FCC to strike down network neutrality in favor of a tiered internet system. In early 2015, Senator Al Franken (D-MN) spoke out about Comcast's lobbying power in the network neutrality debates. He warned that Comcast sought to control regulations on network neutrality for personal business gains. Like others, Comcast was viewed as an opponent of public interest, a company that was viewed as having selfish, profitable interests that compromised public needs.

Comcast was just one of many companies that were identified as opponents to a free and open internet. In a panel on the future of television, former FCC Chair Richard Wiley identified upcoming FCC rulings on network neutrality as a "game-changer" within the television industry. He noted that binge-watching was relevant and a consequence of network neutrality. Corporations were the antithesis of public interest, habits and lifestyles. Leaders then asked their fellow politicians to act against these companies, or stand up to them.

Alternatively, there were other speakers who defended the profit-minded enterprises of large technology companies. Vint Cerf, the Vice President of Google, added that he knew of many politicians who defended his company's right to make money, even when their constituents were opposed to their actions. Although Cerf did not agree with the actions of these politicians (because Google is publicly in favor of network neutrality), his identification and discussion of them denoted their presence.

Throughout this discourse was the close relationship between corporate interests and the workings of Congress. While many political leaders lamented this lobbying effort, it is difficult to tell if this is a true reflection of these speakers' feelings or more a show for the audience. Either way, their verbalized frustrations with the network neutrality issue and its closeness to political leaders were clear.

Politicization

Like the other discourses, it was clear that network neutrality was a pawn in a larger political debate about technology, corporate interference and compromise. However, there were other areas where the issue was politicized as well. For example, for many politicians, jurisdiction of network neutrality was initially unclear. Was it the purview of the FCC, Congress or Judiciary boards? In 1996, Vice President Al Gore addressed Congress and alluded to this confusion. He reflected that he was uncertain who was responsible for it, but he hoped that Congress would protect it. Like earlier speakers who reflected on the lack of understanding of the definition, Gore and others debated the purview of the regulatory system. In a 2012 Town Hall meeting with Senator Ted Cruz (R-TX), he noted that network neutrality is like Obamacare for the internet because of the ability of the President to influence policies on the issue. He argued that the FCC did not have authority to actually rule in favor of network neutrality. This argument, which he echoes here, is actually a continuing theme amongst people who oppose network neutrality: the FCC overstepped and did not have the ability to restrict private enterprise online. Beyond this being emblematic of political stalemate, this type of politicizing the issue was frequent, particularly among Republicans who opposed the FCC's decision.

Constructing Network Neutrality

Throughout the dataset, politicians mostly focused on the implications of network neutrality, rather than the definition or identity. The focus on implications is important because of the message that is communicated to the audience or public. If the politicians, technological leaders and experts on the topic cannot define it, the subject then seems too complicated for public understanding. The message of importance is communicated effectively, but not an actual conceptualization of what it is.

Similar to Powell and Cooper, the four discourses reveal that "local regulatory precedents" contribute to discursive constructions of network neutrality issues in governmental discourse at the state and federal levels. Powell and Cooper (2011) emphasize that the "salient issues" of powerful figures are revealed by close examination of the different ways in which different discourses frame those issues.

To be clear, this is far from a simple Democratic and Republican divide. As the analysis shows, many of the speakers fail to actually understand the topic (and they readily admit to it), but have instead decided to criticize larger political context. Their meta-talk about network neutrality and the political stalemate is actually a type of conscious in Congress. Members agree that there is no agreement. While humorous, this is potentially disastrous to the issue because of the little understanding of its meaning and implications (even though they often focus on implications). For example, while network neutrality may be similar to other digital issues, its frequent combination and equating with cybersecurity is a bit of a stretch. Although frequent, many of the implications for the network neutrality decision are similar to the tenuous relationship with cybersecurity.

Political Speeches and Dialogic Communication

On the surface, political speeches are far from dialogic in nature (perhaps even oppositional), as the public or audience has a limited opportunity to provide feedback or co-construct messaging. Digital dialogic communication requires organizations (in this case, political actors) listen to constituents before making policy decisions or formulating official messages. Political speeches, like the ones identified earlier in this chapter, are often given on the Congressional floor, with limited in-person public audiences. Speeches are a classic type of one-way communication, where the speaker produces messages intended for a listening audience. There is no opportunity for two-way or multimodal communication to take place.

However, in today's digital world, speeches on the Congressional floor go beyond the one-time physical instance and can be reproduced and replayed thousands of times. Each of these speeches was housed on C-SPAN's website, meaning that users have an opportunity to replay each speech, share on other websites, post comments and provide digital feedback. In short, the conversion of each speech into digital formats provides an opportunity for dialogue, particularly if the political actor engages the audience through the platform.

Digital conversion is the act of taking a non-digital artifact, such as a video of a speech, and turning it into a digital file that can be accessed using communication networks such as the internet.[35] While historically the term was used to illustrate how media formats converge into new ones, the act of conversion here means taking a political artifact from an electronic to digital format.[36] Converting political speeches into digital format is a painstaking process enacted by the C-SPAN Archives in order to provide unlimited access to Congressional history for members of the public. Through its mission statement, C-SPAN articulates that the digital database of political speeches intends to provide pathways to engagement between elected officials and the public. Its goals are

> To provide elected and appointed officials and others who would influence public policy a direct conduit to the audience without filtering or otherwise distorting their points of view; To provide the audience, through the call-in program, direct access to elected officials, other decision makers and journalists on a frequent and open basis.[37]

In short, the goal of the archives is to facilitate two-way communication by converting a traditional one-way communication format (speeches).

This two-way communication is indicative of the potential of traditional speeches to motivate and encourage dialogue. The new digital format provides citizens with opportunities to provide feedback and ask questions of political representatives. It also allows political leaders to share messages with the public, respond to inquiries and co-construct public policy. It is the new digital format that allows these processes to take place. The act of digital conversion serves as a gateway for dialogic communication because it changes the type and amount of engagement the public can have with governmental and regulatory speeches and individuals. The political speech, once a one-way communication format, is now a way to begin dialogic communication between political leaders and constituents.

This digital dialogic communication is a way for organizations and political leaders to gauge public opinion, particularly as the public responds to specific political actions (such as the passing of new legislation). Finn notes that political leaders are inclined to use dialogic communication because it helps them create policies and messaging that will be well received by constituents, which is important to reelection motivations.[38] Digital dialogic communication can help leaders construct policies and messages that will incur positive public opinion. So what instances of dialogic communication have emerged from this conversion? In a 2011 speech, Representative Cliff Stearns (R-FL) reflected that public opinion in his district informed much of his conversations with FCC commissioners on network neutrality. Stearns also notes that he uses dialogic communication to engage FCC Commissioners to "hopefully" co-construct policy. He notes, "Any member of Congress can call a Commissioner to his office and most likely he'll come... So you find it's easy to talk to them and it's also helpful in a opening hearing." In Stearns speech, he represents two forms of dialogue that takes place on public policy and on issues such as network neutrality.

First, the videos provide an opportunity for constituents to gain information on representative perspectives as well for public feedback to impact future decisions. In a 2008 interview with Representative Doyle (who later proposed legislation to block the 2017 FCC decision), the Congressman illustrated how he planned to use dialogic communication to engage his constituents in the topic of network neutrality. He reflected, "There is interest in it. Especially those people who are interested in the future of broadband and want to see broadband grow." He goes on to reflect on discussions he's had with Pittsburgh citizens and how he plans to continue these conversations as network neutrality becomes a salient issue. For Doyle, the videos are an opportunity to express his points of view, inform the public and then request feedback from the public as he makes future speeches. His sentiment illustrates the cycle of dialogic communication. While there is no real starting point, in this example, Doyle makes a political speech outlining his point of view, the public watches and interprets his speech, the public provides feedback to Doyle and engages in digital conversations with each other, Doyle receives feedback and updates his point of view/messaging and then Doyle gives his next speech. It is the digital nature of Doyle's speech that motivates the digital dialogic and provides the digital opportunity for the public to discuss his sentiment with each other and provide feedback (Figure 2.1).

Second, dialogic communication takes place between political representatives and the FCC. Although more discussion of the FCC's willingness to take feedback and adjust positioning from politicians or the public is complicated and the focus of Chapter 3, Representatives Stearns's argument, that members of Congress can call the FCC Commissioners to their office at any given time, illustrates that there is a physical moment where two-way communication is possible.

Political Speech

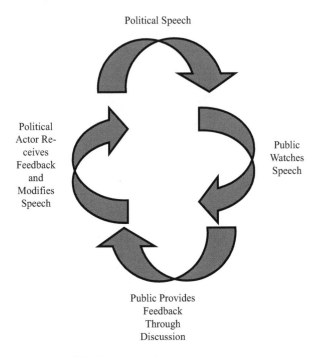

Political
Actor Re-
ceives
Feedback
and
Modifies
Speech

Public
Watches
Speech

Public Provides
Feedback
Through
Discussion

Figure 2.1 Cycle of dialogic communication.

Pieczka argues that this interaction is, by nature, dialogic and focused on building shared mutual understanding and adjusting practices and meaning between parties.[39] While not the same as a public sphere, where many voices are allowed to participate in meaning-building, the act of dialogue between politicians and organizational representatives does articulate symmetrical communication tendencies foundational to relationship management.

For scholars, dialogic communication is important to how political leaders operate and make decisions. Hopper notes that even presidential politics requires two-way communication because of the need to integrate public opinion into initiatives and decisions.[40] For politicians, adopting dialogue processes can mean making policies that are more supported by constituents, thus producing longer elected terms of office.[41] Most scholarship notes that elected officials are compelled to engage in dialogue because they need to galvanize public support. But what happens for government officials and regulators whose job is not determined by elections, but rather appointment. Do they similarly engage in digital dialogues? What compels them to do so? These questions are addressed in the next chapter.

Notes

1 Devin Coldeway, "The FCC Just Repealed Net Neutrality, What Happens Next?" *Tech Crunch*, December 14, 2017. https://beta.techcrunch.com/2017/12/14/the-fcc-just-repealed-net-neutrality-what-happens-next/.
2 US Congressman Mike Doyle, "Members of Congress Condemn FCC Vote to Kill Net Neutrality." December 14, 2017. https://doyle.house.gov/press-release/members-congress-condemn-fcc-vote-kill-net-neutrality.
3 US Congressman Mike Doyle, "Net Neutrality." https://doyle.house.gov/issue/net-neutrality.
4 Ibid.
5 Tracie Mauriello, "Representative Mike Doyle Introduced Legislation to Preserve Net Neutrality." *Pittsburgh Post Gazette*, May 4, 2018. www.postgazette.com/news/nation/2018/02/27/Rep-Mike-Doyle-leads-net-neutrality-effort-in-House-FCC-Democrats-Ajit-Pai/stories/201802270173.
6 Paul Blumenthal, "Democratic Party Think Tank Quietly Fighting Push to Restore Net Neutrality Rules." *Huffington Post*, January 1, 2018. www.huffingtonpost.com/entry/net-neutrality-progressive-policy-institute_us_5a70f13ee4b0be822ba143f4.
7 US Senator Ed Markey, "Senator Markey Leads Resolution to Restore FCC's Net Neutrality Rules." December 14, 2017. www.markey.senate.gov/news/press-releases/senator-markey-leads-resolution-to-restore-fccs-net-neutrality-rules.
8 Ian Bogost, "Network Neutrality Can't Fix the Internet." *The Atlantic*, November 22, 2017. www.theatlantic.com/technology/archive/2017/11/network-neutrality-cant-fix-the-internet/546620/.
9 Alison Powell and Alissa Cooper, "Net Neutrality Discourses: Comparing Advocacy and Regulatory Arguments in the United States and the United Kingdom." *The Information Society* 27, no. 5 (2011): 311–325.
10 Devin Coldeway, "The FCC Just Repealed Net Neutrality, What Happens Next?" *Tech Crunch*, December 14, 2017. https://beta.techcrunch.com/2017/12/14/the-fcc-just-repealed-net-neutrality-what-happens-next/.
11 David D. Clark, "Network Neutrality: Words of Power and 800-pound Gorillas." *International Journal of Communication* 1, no. 1 (2007): 701–708.
12 Ibid., p. 701.
13 Douglas A. Hass, "The Never-Was-Neutral Net and Why Informed End Users Can End the Net Neutrality Debates." *Berkeley Technology Law Journal* 22, no. 4 (2007): 1565–1635; Christine Quail and Christine Larabie, "Net Neutrality: Media Discourses and Public Perception." *Global Media Journal* 3, no. 1 (2010): 31–50.
14 Hsing Kenneth Cheng, Subhajyoti Bandyopadhyay, and Hong Guo, "The Debate on Net Neutrality: A Policy Perspective." *Information Systems Research* 22, no. 1 (2011): 60–82.
15 Emily R. Roxberg, "FCC Authority Post-Comcast: Finding a Happy Medium in the Net Neutrality Debate." *The Journal of Corporation Law* 37, no. 2 (2011): 223.

16 Pramode Verma, "The Elusive Goal of Net Neutrality." *International Journal of Critical Infrastructure Protection* 4, no. 3 (2011): 135–136. doi:10.1016/j.ijcip.2011.09.001.

17 Ibid., p. 135.

18 Christine Quail and Christine Larabie, "Net Neutrality: Media Discourses and Public Perception." *Global Media Journal* 3, no. 1 (2010): 31–50.

19 Peter Dekom, "The Television Wars: Part II: Where's the Neutrality in My Net?" *The Entertainment and Sports Lawyer* 32, no. 1 (2015): 50; Deborah Taylor Tate, "Net Neutrality 10 Years Later: A Still Unconvinced Commissioner." *Federal Communications Law Journal* 66, no. 3 (2014): 509–524.

20 Ajit Pai, "The Story of the FCC's Net Neutrality Decision and Why It Won't Stand Up in Court." *Federal Communications Law Journal* 67, no. 2 (2015): 173.

21 Minjeong Kim, Jang Hyun Kim, and Chung Joo Chung, "Who Shapes Network Neutrality Policy Debate? An Examination of Information Subsidizers in the Mainstream Media and at Congressional and FCC Hearings." *Telecommunications Policy* 35, no. 4 (2011): 315.

22 Ibid., p. 315.

23 Ibid., p. 315.

24 Barbara van Schewick, "Network Neutrality and Quality of Service: What a Nondiscrimination Rule Should Look Like." *Stanford Law Review* 67, no. 1 (2015): 81.

25 Marvin Ammori, "Beyond Content Neutrality: Understanding Content-Based Promotion of Democratic Speech." *Federal Communications Law Journal* 61, no. 2 (2009): 273.

26 Minjeong Kim, Jang Hyun Kim, and Chung Joo Chung, "Who Shapes Network Neutrality Policy Debate? An Examination of Information Subsidizers in the Mainstream Media and at Congressional and FCC Hearings." *Telecommunications Policy* 35, no. 4 (2011): 315.

27 Fred C. Robinson, "The Adoption of Technical Terms in Popular Discourse." *Sewanee Review* 119, no. 2 (2011): 308.

28 Nick Llewellyn, "Audience Participation in Political Discourse: A Study of Public Meetings." *Sociology* 39, no. 4 (2005): 697–716.

29 Fred C. Robinson, "The Adoption of Technical Terms in Popular Discourse." *Sewanee Review* 119, no. 2 (2011): 308.

30 Catherine Fieschi and Paul Heywood, "Trust, Cynicism and Populist Anti-Politics." *Journal of Political Ideologies* 9, no. 3 (2004): 289–309.

31 Tim Wu, *The Master Switch: The Rise and Fall of Information Empires.* First Ed. New York: Alfred A. Knopf, 2010.

32 Tim Wu and Christopher S. Yoo, "Keeping the Internet Neutral?: Tim Wu and Christopher Yoo Debate." *Federal Communications Law Journal* 59, no. 3 (2007): 575.

33 Robin S. Lee and Tim Wu, "Subsidizing Creativity through Network Design: Zero-Pricing and Net Neutrality." *The Journal of Economic Perspectives* 23, no. 3 (2009): 61–76.

34 Tim Wu, *The Master Switch: The Rise and Fall of Information Empires.* First Ed. New York: Alfred A. Knopf, 2010.

35 Lynn, M. Stuart, "Preservation and Access Technology: The Relationship between Digital and Other Media Conversion Processes: A Structured Glossary of Technical Terms." *Information Technology and Libraries* 9, no. 4 (1990): 309.

36 Kiersten F. Latham, "Medium Rare: Exploring Archives and Their Conversion from Original to Digital: Part One: Lessons from the History of Print Media." *LIBRES: Library and Information Science Research Electronic Journal* 20, no. 2 (2010): 1.

37 C-SPAN archives, "About-Mission." www.c-span.org/about/mission/.

38 Jeanine Finn, "Collaborative Knowledge Construction in Digital Environments: Politics, Policy, and Communities." *Government Information Quarterly* 28, no. 3 (2011): 409–415.

39 Magda Pieckza, "Public Relations as Dialogic Expertise?" *Journal of Communication Management* 15, no. 2 (2010):108.

40 Jennifer Hopper, "Obamacare, the News Media, and the Politics of 21st-Century Presidential Communication." *International Journal of Communication (Online)* (2015): 1275.

41 Anders Olof Larsson and Hallvard Moe, "Studying Political Microblogging: Twitter Users in the 2010 Swedish Election Campaign." *New Media & Society* 14, no. 5 (2012): 729–747.

3 FCC and Regulatory Discourses

In May 2017, Federal Communications Commission (FCC) Chairman Ajit Pai posted a three-minute video on YouTube reenacting the well-known segment "Mean Tweets" from Jimmy Kimmel's *Jimmy Kimmel Live!*[1] In the video, Pai read "Mean Tweets" directed toward his Twitter account (@AjitPaiFCC) with humor and short responses. Posted just weeks after he announced FCC intentions to eliminate network neutrality policies, Pai's video was one of the first digital public interactions between the Chairman and audiences. Using the style, layout and even the same backdrop as Jimmy Kimmel's "Mean Tweets" segment, Pai adopted humor to respond to the largely negative public backlash following his network neutrality announcement. Tweets ranged topically, including references to Pai's physique, ego and political leanings. One user wrote, "Ajit Pai is the bad boy wrestler of truthiness that nobody loves to hate. He's a legend in his own mind." Pai responded, while laughing, "yeah" before moving on to the next mean tweet. Throughout the entire segment, Pai used sarcasm to coyly respond to each user and criticism. For example, one user posted with all capitalization: "A. Pai is the Uncle Tom of the Indian people. He is an embarrassment for all non whites. His psychopathic behavior kissing white a** is gross." Pai sarcastically responded, "As a conflicted brown man, I was on the fence, but when you put it in all caps, you persuaded me." Pai's sarcasm serves to degrade the user's concerns and illustrate the innate racism at the core of posts like this one.

Pai's use of sarcasm is almost as prolific as his use of digital media. Since becoming FCC Chairman in January 2017, Pai's tenure was digitally archived through YouTube videos, social media postings, fights with celebrities and even popular magazine interviews.[2] His digital presence differs greatly from the actions of previous chairpersons including Tom Wheeler (who occupied the office just prior to Pai). *The New York Times* notes that traditionally, the FCC is somewhat removed from political and popular life, thus reducing bias and giving it a greater sense of objectivity.[3] Pai, however, took an entirely different approach to his leadership of the office, using digital technology to connect the FCC with citizens. *Quartz* argued that Pai's use of digital media closely mirrored President Donald Trump and even called Pai a "Trump Soldier."[4] The similarities stem from frequent use of social media platforms such as Twitter to informally announce political or policy actions as well as personal reactions and responses to current events. Each man's official Twitter account is a synthesis of both organizational and personal communication. For Pai, this means using social media to post personal reflections, such as favorite pieces of art; respond to popular criticism of his policies; and even announce official changes to FCC organizational structure.[5] Ahmadian et al. reflect that this type of Twitter use seems impulsive and unpredictable to outside audiences, making it valuable for entertainment purposes, but stressful for those who use it to make strategic predictions.

Pai's use of digital media remains at the forefront of popular criticism, steaming beyond the "Mean Tweets" from his YouTube video. Journalistic outlets such as the *New York Times* criticize Pai's efforts to share information digitally using Twitter.[6] However, to Pai, Twitter is a platform to engage the public audience in a way that previous chairpersons were reluctant to do. In fact, all digital media is a means to engage the public in a dialogue about contemporary issues such as network neutrality.

In this sense, Pai uses two-way communication to engage the public in discussion and debate about network neutrality in ways that previous chairpersons did not. His digital media presence provides users with an opportunity to respond by posting, sharing or liking/disliking content. Through videos like "Mean Tweets," Pai responds to users' criticisms and comments, often calling his responses transparent and indicative of his open communication system. And from a surface-level analysis, it does appear that Pai is using digital dialogic communication to engage the public on issues of network neutrality. While audience feedback may not directly change his policies, it does appear to elicit a response, thus signifying two-way communication (but perhaps not mutual adjustment or dialogue). This illustrates a key difference between the enactment of two-way communication and the underlying principle of mutual adjustment in digital dialogic communication. Pai vocalizes responses to users, but fails to integrate their perspective into his strategic decision-making.

There are long-term debates over the role of public opinion and perspective within the FCC. The FCC was founded to serve the public interest; however, the integration of this terminology into practice has a complicated history. Does public feedback represent or serve the public interest? Should the FCC use audience feedback in policymaking? Should they remain objective and removed to make strategic policy choices? FCC history explains how the answers to these questions evolve over time.

FCC History of Audience Engagement

The FCC has a wavering history of audience engagement and the incorporation of public feedback into policymaking. Pickard notes, as far back as the late 1940s, the FCC struggled with the balance of outsider politics and public engagement, questioning regulating technology that connected the masses with politics and its place in the interpretation of policy for everyday audiences.[7] Mora argues that, over time, the FCC struggled to articulate how public feedback was incorporated, if at all, in the policy development process on a number of issues.[8] Because the FCC was often caught between large telecommunication/broadcasting demands and public concerns, the FCC failed to articulate their incorporation of either interest in the development of policy. This did not mean that allegiances to either organizations or the public were invisible throughout history. There are clear examples of FCC allegiance to specific groups (even when loud public protest persisted), such as AT&T in the 1930s and Sinclair Broadcast Group in the 2010s.[9] There are other examples where the FCC clearly revised or updated policy to correspond to public demands and feedback, including the 2015 FCC decision to uphold network neutrality.[10] In short, the FCC inconsistently incorporated public feedback into decisions, reflecting a challenging relationship between the regulatory body and citizens.

Historically, the FCC adopted an objective outsider stance to politics and political bodies.[11] Every President is invited to appoint five FCC commissioners, with no more than three coming from the same political background, and then select one commissioner to serve as chairperson. While the commissioners may not have any financial ties to organizations with any commission-related business, they can lead task forces and committees with representatives from large organizations, advocacy groups and public interest communities.

Despite its close proximity to federal/Presidential politics, the FCC generally does not weigh in on political issues beyond regulatory policies. White argues that although FCC decisions and rulings carry heavy political implications, the office is not supposed to partake in partisan politics and is instead supposed to focus on improving the role of telecommunication in public interest.[12] The phrase "public interest" is perhaps the most challenging part of the FCC's mission because it requires each chairperson to conceptualize "public" against the contemporary sociocultural backdrop. Obar and Schejter note that for some commissioners, this means promoting policies of regulation that motivate competition between organizations and thus reduce costs and improve opportunities for members of the public.[13] For others, it means promoting policies of deregulation that consolidate power among a few telecommunication industries and improve profitability and shareholder value. Tim Wu refers to this as the oscillation between large monopolistic organizations and smaller regulated ones that has occurred since the start of the 20th century.[14] In periods of deregulation, companies combine with each other to form monopolies with dominating control within a communications medium. During periods of regulation, these companies are broken apart and new organizations form to take advantage of the competitive environment. For Obar and Schejter, this oscillation is often a result of FCC leadership and changes in the conceptualization of "public interest."

Public interest or "public interest standard" originated from the 1927 Radio Act (which predated the creation of the FCC). This act gave "federal regulators the power to regulate if they found it was in the 'public interest, convenience, or necessity.'"[15] This vague description is problematic because it fails to provide specific instructions on what actions benefit or harm the public interest. Nobel Laureate economist Ronald Coase reflected, "The phrase... lacks any definite meaning. Furthermore, the many inconsistencies in commission decisions have made it impossible for the phrase to acquire a definite meaning in the process of regulation."[16] This has produced inconsistent definitions of "public interest" over time, thus allowing commissioners to use it to benefit a variety of stakeholders in the policymaking process.[17] The Foundation for Economic Education adds that the "standard has become a non-standard," and that the phrase has "no fixed meaning" that helps commissioners or public audiences conceptualize policy impact.[18]

Thus, "public interest" was used by commissioners to promote both regulatory and deregulatory policies. For example, in the 1960s, the public interest standard was used to promote policies that stifled the development of cable television at the request of existing broadcasters. Kellogg et al. argue, "For many years the FCC's principal objective was to suppress the cable industry by preventing direct competition between cable, and over-the-air broadcasting. It did so quite successfully."[19] Hazlett argues that this slowed down the rate of cable innovation dramatically, thus giving traditional broadcasters a competitive advantage for nearly a decade.[20] Despite commissioners citing the "public interest standard" when defending the regulation of cable, little evidence demonstrates that the policy upheld the public interest at all. For Hazlett, the "public interest standard" became a vacant phrase that was used to frame policies as "publicly beneficial" even when they clearly stagnated innovation and competition that might benefit citizens.

There are limits to the "public interest standard" and the FCC's ability to regulate communication media. The First Amendment, which promises free speech to citizens, limits the extensive ability of the FCC. *Current* argues,

> The Federal Government may not censor broadcasters, for example, nor may it regulate content except in the most general fashion, including favoring broad categories of programming such as public affairs and local programming. The FCC can intervene to correct perceived inadequacies in overall industry performance, but it cannot trample on the broad editorial discretion of licensees.[21]

In short, while the FCC can make large regulatory policies regarding how organizations operate (and whom they operate with), they cannot stifle or hinder free speech.

Chao reflects that the interpretation of "public interest" changed dramatically in the 1980s, against the backdrop of Reagan's deregulations.[22]

> FCC Chairman Mark Fowler, appointed by President Ronald Reagan, decided that the public interest was sufficiently addressed by free market conditions and did not merit government safeguards. In short, the public would demonstrate its interests through active viewership and advertisers would respond accordingly with revenue dollars supporting the programs with the most 'public interest.' Programs without sufficient 'public interest' would cease production without sufficient advertising dollars to support it as a result of market efficiencies. The public interest became essentially 'what interests the public.' Under this approach, the FCC did away with programming guidelines, commercial limits, and community needs ascertainment, though it maintained some regulatory requirements over educational content for children.[23]

Known as the "efficiency interpretation" of "public interest standard," this produced deregulation in the 1980s. Chao argues that Chairman

Pai similarly uses the efficiency interpretation to motivate a late-2010 period of deregulation.

Importantly, the efficiency interpretation holds ramifications for both the First Amendment and digital dialogic communication.[24] As Chao reflects,

> It is alarming to see the FCC prioritize market efficiency and corporate interests over a healthy, diverse marketplace of ideas, particularly because the latter is a fundamental pillar for any democracy. Without a diversity of viewpoints, a community's ability to actively enable people's participation in public discourse and democracy as equals is hindered, as bigger media conglomerates gain access to wider platforms to disseminate their positions.[25]

In short, periods of deregulation prioritize larger organizations over smaller ones, thus limiting smaller organizations from engaging the public and using dialogic communication to facilitate feedback and discussion.

Ali argues that this change in FCC definition of "public interest" evolved over time, and actions during Pai's leadership were a product of nearly 30 years of deregulation: "Over the last 30 years, America's communications regulators have moved away from focusing on society's benefit, and toward an interpretation of the public interest as equivalent to what businesses want."[26] Former FCC Chairman Nicholas Johnson warns that this trend results in a diminished ability of public groups to communicate and engage each other digitally. He reflects,

> Whatever is your first priority, whether it is women's rights or saving wildlife, your second priority has to be media reform. With it you at least have a chance of accomplishing your first priority. Without it, you don't have a prayer.[27]

In the past, public groups have used online communication to confront policies that limit or hinder "public interest," such as in 2003 when the FCC attempted to change media ownership rules. Within three days, nearly three million citizens contacted the FCC to reject the changes, prompting the FCC to reconsider.[28] This digital engagement was enacted through policies of network neutrality, meaning all citizens had equal access to the FCC commenting system. Ali notes that if network neutrality policies are eliminated, organizations could stifle or slow down access to the same FCC commenting system, thus hindering the ability to provide and receive feedback and engage dialogic practices.[29]

It is not just the "public interest standard" that complicates the FCC's history of audience engagement and feedback on proposed policies. There are currently no policies that enforce how much audience feedback must be considered in policy decisions. Although the FCC invites public feedback on policy proposals, comments can be dismissed for a variety of reasons. In fact, most comments are dismissed if they singularly contain "opinions" versus facts or legal arguments.[30] In short, the FCC "comprehensively addresses all the serious comments that made factual and legal arguments" but not comments that seem to singularly convey an individual's opinion.[31] Velazco reflects that there is nothing that forces the FCC to consider public comments or even take into consideration public opinion when making decisions, even when survey and poll data overwhelmingly support an opposite set of actions.[32]

Brown and Blevins argue that historically, the FCC has not used public opinion to drive many policy decisions.[33] In actuality, most FCC leaders argue that public opinion stifles the ability to create and enforce objective policies, thus opting to ignore public feedback and opinions. Cole and Oettinger reflect,

> In the past, the FCC has been a tight little world in which commissioners enjoyed many personal contacts with the broadcasters they regulated (and their lawyers and lobbyists) and none at all with the amorphous public whose interests the agency supposedly protected[34]

However, public protest and anger directed toward commissioners who failed to listen to the public motivated some early forms of public engagement. For example, Commissioner Michael Copps held a series of public meetings around the country to "challenge FCC's proposals to revise or repeal a series of broadcast ownership rules that limited further consolidation, especially in the broadcast television sector." This is one early example where public opinion was used to inform policy actions. However, as noted by Brown and Blevins, this is an outlier to a particularly insulated world, where the FCC rarely uses public opinion and feedback in decisions.

Chairman Wheeler's leadership during the 2015 consideration of network neutrality seemingly stands opposed to the historical exclusion of public opinion in policy decision-making. In 2015, Chairman Wheeler vocalized appreciation for public feedback through the FCC commenting system, reflecting that the public opinion motivated his beliefs. Wheeler's own background proved surprising for some members of the public who anticipated a different stance on network neutrality. One citizen wrote,

> If you told me 5 years ago that a 20-year lobbyist veteran would be named the head of the FCC and reclassify the wired and wireless internet agencies under Title II, I'd have punched you in the arm and called you a f***ing liar. I have never been more happy to be proven wrong about a book's cover than I have been with Mr. Wheeler.[35]

In a 2017 interview with former Chairman Wheeler, *Fast Company* called his 2015 network neutrality legislation the defining moment of his career, despite the reversal of this policy in 2017.[36] Wheeler defended the autonomy of the FCC from the White House during his tenure, arguing that under Pai's leadership, the FCC has become a political mechanism for the Trump administration. He reflected,

> The fact that the chairman was summoned to talk to the president in the Oval Office and won't talk about what they talked about … I can assure you Barack Obama never summoned *me* to his office. You just have to worry about things like that.[37]

For Wheeler, public opinion was a way to gain insight into the future reception of regulatory policies. The FCC commenting system was an opportunity to engage the public in conversation about ongoing policy debates and adjust FCC policies to fit this feedback. While Wheeler failed to acknowledge the direct role that the commenting system had in his support of network neutrality, he argued that it was a fundamental process to understanding what is in the "public interest."

Wheeler became the target of many of the comments posted in 2014 and 2015, particularly after John Oliver identified him as a problematic leader of the FCC. Oliver cited Wheeler's history of lobbying for the cable industry as a possible reason for the slow movement on network neutrality: Wheeler's appointment as FCC Chairman is "the equivalent of needing a babysitter and hiring a dingo." As Oliver's segment gained popularity, Wheeler voiced his support for network neutrality and even thanked Oliver: "Well, I became a cult figure…Actually, it helped raise the visibility of the whole thing. And it certainly created a strange sensation for me where suddenly the head of this small agency was [well] known."[38] While the public engagement with the issue was likely only one part of Wheeler's decision to support network neutrality, he did cite it as important to the overall acceptance of the policy and future attempts to repeal or reform.[39] In short, Wheeler used public opinion to justify and inform his own stance on the policy and motivate network neutrality policy actions in 2015.

Ajit Pai served as an FCC commissioner under Chairman Tom Wheeler during the 2015 network neutrality decision. Just months before his 2017 appointment as Chairman by the new President Trump, Pai argued for a new period of deregulation: "We need to fire up the weed whacker and remove those rules that are holding back investment, innovation and job creation."[40] Pai's history as Verizon Communication's General Council from 2001 to 2003 demonstrates his position as a free market advocate and "formidable opponent for public interest groups," according to Schwartzman.[41]

Pai stood out in 2015 as a critic of network neutrality, particularly arguing that the terms of the FCC's policymaking were opaque and unethical. Pai famously filmed himself holding the 332-page network neutrality proposal that was held confidential by Chairman Tom Wheeler before the FCC vote. Pai wanted the proposal to be publicly available before the commissioner vote, arguing that the public needed to know the full scope of proposed regulations. Pai reflected, "I believe the public has a right to know what its government is doing, particularly when it comes to something as important as Internet regulation."[42] In the same 45-minute speech, Pai repeatedly called the proposal "President Obama's plan to regulate the Internet" and alluded to Chairman Wheeler's speech as "spin." He concluded, "We need to make this plan public so that the American people can make a decision for themselves." While FCC spokesperson Hart responded citing the long-standing policy of privacy for FCC proposals and Chairman Wheeler added he had no intentions of publicizing the proposal, Pai's speech was indicative of his larger position that the FCC existed in too much secrecy. Pai demanded more transparency in the FCC, including publicizing regulatory policies before FCC votes in order to gain feedback from citizens and impacted groups. Two years later, Pai was appointed Chairman and promised to undo Chairman Wheeler's regulations all while using social media to engage the public.

William Brangham, from PBS News, argues that Pai's stance on network neutrality is relatively simple: network neutrality is indicative of Obama-era regulations that limited corporate growth and pro-business agendas.[43] To succeed and undo or eliminate network neutrality, Pai would be responsible for the largest period of growth in corporate digital power, and upend Obama's legacy. Eliminating network neutrality was one of Pai's priorities as he took office in 2017. In his December 2017 announcement, Pai called the 2015 policy "micromanagement" by federal government of corporate behavior.[44] Thus, his repeal of network neutrality would eliminate the micromanagement of the Obama era. On the day of his December 2017 announcement about eliminating network neutrality, Pai tweeted, "Today, I'm proposing to repeal the heavy-handed Internet regulations imposed by the Obama Administration and to return to the light-touch framework under which the Internet developed and thrived before 2015."[45] Pai frequently refers to network neutrality as a relic of the "Obama era" and "Obama administration," despite it originating from the FCC, not the President (although President Obama did voice support for the policy).

Pai's frequent invocation of President Obama is not the only common element of his speeches and public dialogue. The *Los Angeles Times* critiqued Pai's speeches after his 2017 appointment and argued that Pai uses the opportunity to brag about his social media skills and popular culture knowledge.[46] Griff's argues that Pai uses references to topics such as baseball and Batman as a bridge to public policy and a way to demonstrate that his policies would align with mass public interests.[47] However, far from being well-received, Pai's references are often rejected by members of the public on social media as shallow or inauthentic public appeals. For example, on March 6, 2018, Pai tweeted out his appreciation for the 20th anniversary of the debut of *The Big Lebowski*: "It's not just, like, my opinion, man: 20 years ago today, #TheBigLebowski – the greatest film in the history of cinema – was released. Decades on, the Dude still abides and the movie really ties us all together."[48] *Complex* magazine questioned Pai's continued references to popular culture items, like the cult-classic film *The Big Lebowski*:

> Perhaps in an attempt to rebuild his image or connect with his followers (who I assume are mostly hate-follows), Pai praised the Coen Brothers film on its 20th birthday in a tweet that was quickly dragged to filth by the masses.[49]

Pai's popular culture references are often critiqued by members of the public who are frustrated by his attempts to appeal to popular culture. For example, Twitter users responded with "Funny how you're trying to pander to the people you're screwing over by ending net neutrality. We see you and we think you're repellent. Delete your account, it's not like you need it." and "I was going to rent The Big Lebowski on Amazon, but my cable provider will end up throttling it and make it unwatchable. Thanks Ajit!!!"

Pai's Twitter account is used for both official FCC business and personal reflections, making it the target of angry users who are frustrated by Pai's stance or FCC policies. Beyond Twitter, Pai uses YouTube and other digital media platforms to share information and engage the public. For example, in December 2017, just a week after Pai's vote to eliminate network neutrality, Pai posted a one-minute video on YouTube called "7 things you can still do on the Internet after net neutrality."[50] The video contained a list of seven items (reenacted by Pai) people frequently do on the internet, including Instagramming pictures of food (Pai shown taking selfies of sriracha and flaming Cheetos), posting pictures of cute animals, shopping for "X-mas" presents (Pai shown buying a bulk order of fidget spinners), binge-watching your favorite shows and staying part of your favorite fandom (Pai shown holding a lightsaber with thematic *Star Wars* music in the background).

Users watching the YouTube video were quick to post replies, most of which were negative. For example, "he's trying so hard to be hip. Someone send him a pack of bees." and

> This is so insultingly condescending. Is this all you think we use the internet for? We use the internet to run our businesses. We use it to telework. We use it monitor our homes. We use it to track our finances. We use it to manage our health care. You boiled it down to wanting to 'Gram our food.' You are a total moron.

Clearly, users were upset by Pai's belittling of the impact of network neutrality and his attempt to use popular culture to persuade audiences to understand and support his decision.

Later the same month, conservative newsite *The Daily Caller* posted a second video of Pai responding to network neutrality criticism while dancing to the "Harlem Shake," holding a lightsaber and posing with Pizzagate conspiracy theorist Martina Markota.[51] *The Verge* called the video "flippant" and "unpopular," while the DJ responsible for producing the "Harlem Shake" soundtrack appealed to YouTube to pull down the video for copyright infringement.[52] After several hours, *The Daily Caller* convinced Google and YouTube to reinstate the video on the site. However, once the video reappeared, criticism started rolling in, as it had in response to his first video.[53]

The public responded to the videos using a variety of platforms beyond YouTube comments. This included an unfortunate incident where an Indian DJ named Ajit Pai received thousands of angry comments on Instagram shortly after the first video debuted.[54] With the exception of mistaken identity, Pai's use of social media allows an opportunity for citizens to provide feedback and insight to him on a variety of topics, including popular culture. However, in most cases, his posts receive negative feedback from traditional users, including a series of death threats.[55]

Even journalists and large news publications have critiqued Pai's approach to popular culture and citizen outreach. In addition to appearing inauthentic and pandering, journalists identify one group that is often subtly at the center of Pai's content: the Millennial Generation. *Vanity Fair* argued, "Pai has a history of using embarrassing videos to ingratiate himself with skeptical millennials."[56]*Slate* magazine argued that Pai's videos pantomime millennial habits, such as taking selfies with food, binging television shows and popularizing trending toys like the fidget spinner. However, the purpose of these references is under debate with several interpretations of his motivations. First, by invoking these items in his videos, Pai may want people to see him as connected and aware of popular culture, and aligned with the largest demographic group in the country. Or, more likely, according to Gentlemen's Quarterly (*GQ*), "It certainly looks like he's just trolling his critics and pretending their complaints are petty millennial nonsense that he never intended to take seriously." According to National Public Radio (NPR), Pai's videos are similar to dog whispers, where his insults are so vague that they could simply be misunderstood as genuine yet poor attempts to connect with the audience.[57]

But why would Pai want to bait the Millennial Generation, or even care about their reception of his new policies? *Nielsen Reports* argue that millennials are the most active generational group on digital media and are responsible for the highest consumption of nontraditional cable television broadcasting.[58] This means that millennials seek out alternative ways to consume television programs, such as Apple TV, Roku and PlayStation. Bloom reflects that network neutrality means more to millennials because they spend more of their life on digital platforms. Also, historically millennials were influential in the 2015 network neutrality decision and were responsible for more posts in the FCC commenting system than any other group.[59] Thus, their continued interest in the policy makes them a salient group to the FCC. Aside from journalistic interpretations, there is limited scholarly work that looks at millennial responses to Pai's videos and use of digital media. However, politically, democrats hope millennial support for network neutrality will continue throughout upcoming elections, particularly as it is egged on by Pai's subtly insulting videos and references.[60] The long-term impact, however, remains to be seen.

Despite Pai's prolific use of social media for personal and official purposes, there is little indication that public opinion and the feedback offered on each platform are used by Pai (or the FCC) to guide decisions. While Pai clearly articulated his goals of repealing network neutrality in 2015 if given the opportunity, his messaging and responses do not demonstrate a digital dialogic. Kent and Taylor argue that dialogic communication "involves an effort to recognize the value of the other [impacted members of the public]."[61] Pai's continual subtle insults of the Millennial Generation prevent him from recognizing possible value in public concerns. By poking fun at millennial trends and habits, Pai does not practice the empathy required in digital dialogic communication, and fails to recognize millennial insights into network neutrality as valuable.

However, Pai's non-dialogic behaviors seemingly contradict his earlier expressed interests in making the FCC more transparent and open to public insight. His criticisms of Chairman Wheeler's secrecy surrounding the 2015 proposal indicated that he planned on providing more opportunities for public feedback if he was appointed to the position later on. He describes his own use of social media as a way to interact and engage the public, all while denying the core principle of "value" within the digital dialogic.

In this sense, Pai illustrates the illusion of a digital dialogic, one where he claims that his use of digital media is a mechanism to engage the public and elicit feedback, but fails to follow up and actually perform the task of mutual adjustment. Public feedback serves no real function in the creation of policy for Chairman Pai, but rather has a self-serving function to create the illusion that public feedback is used. Digital engagement is a type of branding opportunity to Pai, not a series of dialogic processes that may influence and shape decision-making and messaging.

Despite the illusion of digital dialogic communication taking place through Pai's social media, Pai remains committed to using information gained through the FCC Public Commenting system, even extending the commenting window to allow for additional feedback.[62] However, it is clear from Pai's official responses to these comments that legal and political content is prioritized over opinions. When extending the commenting window in 2017, Pai noted that this was only done so legal scholars could have additional time to build and inform arguments, not so that additional public opinion could be garnered.[63] Again, extensions like these provide an illusion of dialogic, rather than true inquiries for public feedback.

The illusion of a digital dialogic is powerful, especially because it holds the potential to influence the public's perception of their own impact in the policymaking process. If successful, the illusion makes the public think that they are a larger part of the process than they really are and that their feedback and opinions are useful and valuable in decision-making. Thus far, there is little evidence that Pai's digital dialogic illusion is successful, particularly as journalists and users continue to criticize his efforts and digital presence.

However, there are moments when it appears that digital feedback may hold some impact on Pai's messaging and communication initiatives. For example, in January 2018, Pai declined an invitation to speak at the Consumer Electronics Show in Las Vegas, even though it would have been an opportunity to speak without questions or audience input. Instead, he sent colleagues from the FCC to the event to host a roundtable discussion with members of the public and large telecommunication organizations.[64] Although a roundtable discussion is not a commitment to use public feedback while making decisions, the change in format from speech to discussion illustrates that perhaps there are opportunities to provide public input and feedback.

As with Pai's social media use, his inconsistent approach to using public feedback in policy creation is anxiety-producing for stakeholders interested in predicting upcoming actions and decisions. For organizations seeking to engage and influence policy creation, public feedback is fundamentally important to constructing policies that will be supported by consumers. The next chapter illustrates how organizations have sought to influence the policy development process, particularly as telecommunication companies that can both shape network neutrality and be shaped by it.

Notes

1 Independent Journal Review, "Ajit Pai Reads Mean Tweets." *YouTube*, May 13, 2017. www.youtube.com/watch?v=iBt84HNAGwU.
2 Olivia Solon, "The Man Who Could Doom Net Neutrality: Ajit Pai Ignores Outcry from all Sides." *The Guardian*, December 7, 2017. www.theguardian.com/technology/2017/dec/07/net-neutrality-fcc-ajit-pai.
3 Tiffany Hsu, "Doing the Harlem Shake, Ajit Pai as You've Never Seen Him before." *The New York Times*, December 15, 2017. www.nytimes.com/2017/12/15/business/ajit-pai-video.html.
4 Heather Timmons, "Who Is Ajit Pai, the 'Trump Soldier' Coming for Your Internet?" *Quartz*, December 14, 2017. https://qz.com/1133973/net-neutrality-who-is-ajit-pai-the-trump-soldier-coming-for-your-internet/.
5 Sara Ahmadian, Sara Azarshahi, and Delroy L. Paulhus, "Explaining Donald Trump via Communication Style: Grandiosity, Informality, and Dynamism." *Personality and Individual Differences* 107 (2017): 49–53.

6 Tiffany Hsu, "Doing the Harlem Shake, Ajit Pai as You've Never Seen Him before." *The New York Times*, December 15, 2017. www.nytimes.com/2017/12/15/business/ajit-pai-video.html.
7 Victor Pickard, "The Battle over the FCC Blue Book: Determining the Role of Broadcast Media in a Democratic Society, 1945–8." *Media, Culture & Society* 33, no. 2 (2011): 171–191.
8 G. Cristina Mora, "Regulating Immigrant Media and Instituting Ethnic Boundaries – The FCC and Spanish-Language Television: 1960–1990." *Latino Studies* 9, no. 2–3 (2011): 242–262.
9 Gwen Lisa Shaffer and Scott Jordan, "Classic Conditioning: The FCC's Use of Merger Conditions to Advance Policy Goals." *Media, Culture & Society* 35, no. 3 (2013): 392–403.
10 Matthew Howard, *Net Neutrality for Broadband: Understanding the FCC's 2015 Open Internet Order*. New York: Puma Concolor Aeternus Press, 2015: 15.
11 Evan R. Kwerel and Gregory L. Rosston, "An Insiders' View of FCC Spectrum Auctions." *Journal of Regulatory Economics* 17, no. 3 (2000): 253–289.
12 Candace White, 'Activist Efforts of the Center for Media and Democracy to Affect FCC Policy for Video News Releases." *Public Relations Review* 38, no. 1 (2012): 76–82.
13 Jonathan A. Obar and Amit M. Schejter, "Inclusion or Illusion? An Analysis of the FCC's Public Hearings on Media Ownership 2006–2007." *Journal of Broadcasting & Electronic Media* 54, no. 2 (2010): 212–227.
14 Tim Wu, *The Master Switch: The Rise and Fall of Information Empires*. First Ed. New York: Alfred A. Knopf, 2010.
15 Adam Thierer, "Is the Public Served by the Public Interest Standard?" *Foundation for Economic Education*, September 1, 1996. https://fee.org/articles/is-the-public-served-by-the-public-interest-standard/.
16 Ronald H. Coase, "The Federal Communications Commission." *The Journal of Law and Economics* 2 (October 1959): 8–9.
17 William T. Mayton, "The Illegitimacy of the Public Interest Standard at the FCC." *Emory Law Journal* 38 (1989): 715–769.
18 Adam Thierer, "Is the Public Served by the Public Interest Standard?" *Foundation for Economic Education*, September 1, 1996. https://fee.org/articles/is-the-public-served-by-the-public-interest-standard/.
19 Michael K. Kellogg, John Thorne, and Peter W. Huber, *Federal Telecommunications Law*. Boston: Little, Brown, 1992: 689.
20 Thomas W. Hazlett, "Station Brakes: The Government's Campaign against Cable Television." *Reason* 26, no. 9 (February 1995): 41–47.
21 Current, "The Public Interest Standard in Television Broadcasting." *Current: News for People in Public Media*, December 18, 1998. https://current.org/1998/12/the-public-interest-standard-in-television-broadcasting/.
22 Becky Chao, "The Value of the FCC's Public Interest Mandate in Empowering Community Voices." *New America*, December 14, 2017. www.newamerica.org/millennials/dm/value-fccs-public-interest-mandate-empowering-community-voices/.
23 Ibid.
24 Haeryon Kim, "The Politics of Deregulation: Public Participation in the FCC Rulemaking Process for DBS." *Telecommunications Policy* 19, no. 1 (1995): 51–60.

25 Becky Chao, "The Value of the FCC's Public Interest Mandate in Empowering Community Voices." *New America*, December 14, 2017. www.newamerica.org/millennials/dm/value-fccs-public-interest-mandate-empowering-community-voices/.

26 Christopher Ali, "Trump's FCC Continues to Redefine the Public Interest as Business Interest." *The Conversation*, March 28, 2017. http://theconversation.com/trumps-fcc-continues-to-redefine-the-public-interest-as-business-interests-75120.

27 Nicholas Johnson, *Your Second Priority*. New York: Lulu, 2008.

28 Timothy Karr, "Public Interest Groups Respond to New FCC Ownership Rules." *Save the Internet*, June 21, 2006. www.savetheinternet.com/release/156.

29 Christopher Ali, "Trump's FCC Continues to Redefine the Public Interest as Business Interest." *The Conversation*, March 28, 2017. http://theconversation.com/trumps-fcc-continues-to-redefine-the-public-interest-as-business-interests-75120.

30 Jon Brodkin, "FCC Explains Why Public Support for Net Neutrality Won't Stop It's Repeal." *ArsTechnica*, November 22, 2017. https://arstechnica.com/tech-policy/2017/11/why-the-fcc-ignored-public-opinion-in-its-push-to-kill-net-neutrality/.

31 Ibid.

32 Chris Velazo, "The FCC Doesn't Care What You Think About Net Neutrality." *Edgenet*, April 27, 2014. www.engadget.com/2017/04/27/the-fcc-doesn-t-care-what-you-think-about-net-neutrality/.

33 Duncan H. Brown and Jeffrey Layne Blevins, "Can the FCC Still Ignore the Public?: Interviews with Two Commissioners Who Listened." *Television & New Media* 9, no. 6 (2008): 447–470.

34 Barry Cole and Mal Oettinger, *Reluctant Regulators: The FCC and the Broadcast Audience*. Reading, MA: Addison-Wesley, 1978.

35 Jon Brodkin, "Tom Wheeler Defeats the Broadband Industry: Net Neutrality Wins in Court." *Ars Technica*, June 14, 2017. https://arstechnica.com/tech-policy/2016/06/net-neutrality-and-title-ii-win-in-court-as-isps-lose-case-against-fcc/.

36 Chris Velazo, "The FCC Doesn't Care What You Think about Net Neutrality." *Edgenet*, April 27, 2014. www.engadget.com/2017/04/27/the-fcc-doesn-t-care-what-you-think-about-net-neutrality/.

37 Mark Sullivan, "Ex-FCC Chair Tom Wheeler Dismantles the Case for Abandoning Net Neutrality." *Fast Company*, July 31, 2017. www.fastcompany.com/40445949/ex-chair-tom-wheeler-dismantles-fccs-argument-to-abandon-net-neutrality.

38 Ted Johnson, "Tom Wheeler Interview: FCC Chairman Says Rolling Back Agenda Will Be 'Easier Said than Done'." *Variety*, January 13, 2017. http://variety.com/2017/biz/news/tom-wheeler-fcc-1201960235/.

39 Jacob Kastrenekes, "Outgoing FCC Chief Tom Wheeler Offers Final Defense of Net Neutrality." *The Verge*, January 13, 2017. www.theverge.com/2017/1/13/14266168/tom-wheeler-final-speech-net-neutrality-defense.

40 Jim Puzzangehera, "Trump Names New FCC Chairman: Ajit Pai, Who Wants to Take a 'weed Whacker' to Net Neutrality." *Los Angeles Times*, January 23, 2017. www.latimes.com/business/la-fi-pai-fcc-chairman-20170123-story.html.

41 Ibid.

42 Jim Puzzangehera, "FCC's Pai: Net Neutrality Proposal Is Secret Internet Regulation Plan." *Los Angeles Times*, February 10, 2015. www.latimes.com/business/la-fi-net-neutrality-fcc-ajit-pai-tom-wheeler-20150210-story.html.

43 Judy Roodruff, "FCC Chair Ajit Pai Explains Why He Wants to Scrap Net Neutrality." *PBS Newshour*, April 27, 2017. www.pbs.org/newshour/show/fcc-chair-ajit-pai-explains-wants-scrap-net-neutrality.

44 Brian Fung, "FCC Plan Would Give Internet Providers Power to Choose the Sites Customers See and Use." *The Washington Post*, November 21, 2017. www.washingtonpost.com/news/the-switch/wp/2017/11/21/the-fcc-has-unveiled-its-plan-to-rollback-its-net-neutrality-rules/?utm_term=.0812248dafcd.

45 Jeffrey Cook and Stephanie Ebbs, "FCC Looks to Repeal Obama-era Net Neutrality Rules." *ABC News*, November 21, 2017. http://abcnews.go.com/US/fcc-repeal-obama-era-net-neutrality-rules/story?id=51309157.

46 Jim Puzzangehera, "Trump Names New FCC Chairman: Ajit Pai, Who Wants to Take a 'Weed Whacker' to Net Neutrality." *Los Angeles Times*, January 23, 2017. www.latimes.com/business/la-fi-pai-fcc-chairman-20170123-story.html.

47 Kelce Griffs, "For FCC's Pai, Pop Culture Is a Bridge to Policy." *Law360*, August 8, 2017. www.law360.com/articles/951915/for-fcc-s-pai-pop-culture-is-a-bridge-to-policy.

48 Clayton Purdom, "Ajit Pai Will Not Rest until He Has Ruined the Big Lebowski." *AV Club*, March 6, 2018. www.avclub.com/ajit-pai-will-not-rest-until-he-has-ruined-the-big-lebo-1823549081.

49 Sarah Jasmine Montgomery, "Internet's Least Favorite Person, Ajit Pai Tries Praising Internet's Favorite Movie the Big Lebowski." *Complex*, March 6, 2018. www.complex.com/pop-culture/2018/03/ajit-pai-tries-praising-internet-favorite-movie-the-big-lebowski/.

50 Mitchell Wiggs, "FCC Chairman Ajit Pai Explains Net Neutrality." December 14, 2017. www.youtube.com/watch?v=JqONIPwidQw.

51 Sarah Jeong, "Youtube Briefly Took Down FCC Chairman AJit Pai." *The Verge*, December 16, 2017. www.theverge.com/2017/12/16/16785190/youtube-took-down-fcc-chairman-ajit-pai-mad-decent-harlem-shake.

52 Ibid.

53 Jacqueline Thomson, "'Harlem Shake' Creators Threaten to Sue over FCC Chair's Anti-Net Neutrality Video." *The Hill*, December 15, 2017. http://thehill.com/blogs/in-the-know/in-the-know/365061-harlem-shake-creators-threaten-to-sue-over-fcc-chairmans-anti.

54 Megan Farokhmanesh, "A DJ Named Ajit Pai's Had a Bad Day on Instagram." *The Verge*, December 14, 2017. www.theverge.com/2017/12/14/16777596/dj-ajit-pai-bad-day-instagram.

55 Tony Perkins, "Death Threats against FCC Chairman Are Unprecidented and Must Stop." *Daily Signal*, January 10, 2018. http://dailysignal.com/2018/01/10/death-threats-fcc-chairman-unprecedented-must-stop/.

56 Maya Koseoff, *"Trump FCC Chairman: Destroying Net Neutrality Is Actually Fun and Cool." Vanity Fair*, December 14, 2017. www.vanityfair.com/news/2017/12/trump-fcc-chairman-destroying-net-neutrality-is-actually-fun-and-cool.

57 Brian Naylor, "As FCC Prepares Net Neutrality Vote, Study Finds Millions of Fake Comments." *NPR*, December 14, 2017. www.npr.org/2017/12/14/570262688/as-fcc-prepares-net-neutrality-vote-study-finds-millions-of-fake-comments.

58 David Bloom, "Why Ajit Pai's Net Neutrality Changes Mean More to Millennials." *Tube Filler*, April 28, 2018. www.tubefilter.com/2017/04/28/ajit-pai-fcc-net-neutrality-millennials/.

59 Konrad Von Finckenstein and Peter Menzies, "Millennial Moment: Will the Tech Generation Fight for Net Neutrality?" *The Globe and Mail*, November 27, 2017. www.theglobeandmail.com/report-on-business/rob-commentary/millennial-moment-will-the-tech-generation-fight-for-net-neutrality/article37094897/.

60 Reuters, "Net Neutrality Repeal Gives US Democrats a Fresh Way to Reach Millennials." *Japan Times*, December 15, 2017. www.japantimes.co.jp/news/2017/12/15/business/tech/net-neutrality-repeal-gives-u-s-democrats-fresh-way-reach-millennials/#.WqbezOgbNPY.

61 Michael L. Kent and Maureen Taylor, "Toward a Dialogic Theory of Public Relations." *Public Relations Review* 28, no. 1 (2002): 22.

62 Sanford D. Bishop, "Section 706 NOI." *FCC*, October 24, 2017. https://apps.fcc.gov/edocs_public/attachmatch/DOC-347600A1.pdf.

63 Ibid.

64 Jake Johnson, "Cowardice: Ajit Pai Accused of Hiding from Net Neutrality Backers after Bailing on Tech Conference." *Common Dreams*, January 4, 2018. www.commondreams.org/news/2018/01/04/cowardice-ajit-pai-accused-hiding-net-neutrality-backers-after-bailing-tech.

4 Organizational and Industrial Interpretations

In 2014, Comcast Corporation, one of the largest telecommunication organizations in the world, unveiled a pledge to uphold the principles of network neutrality and reject internet fast lanes. Housed on its "Net Neutrality" page, the organization loudly promoted the policy and stance, arguing that this type of company-wide policy protected consumers and solidified the organization's ethical principles and philosophy. However, on April 26, 2017, Comcast's pledge unexpectedly disappeared from its official website.[1] What caused this dramatic change and shift in Comcast's publicized stance on network neutrality? While the organization never admitted a correlation, the change occurred just hours after Federal Communications Commission (FCC) Chairman Pai announced plans to eliminate network neutrality rules. Journalists criticized the timing of Comcast's policy pivot and suspected the shift resulted from the FCC's announcement, not larger organizational philosophical changes.[2]

Organizations have a stake in FCC decisions on network neutrality. For large organizations, eliminating the policy means intensified competition between companies vying for public attention and access. Larger organizations with greater digital budgets can pay for internet fast lanes and prioritized access to consumers. Smaller organizations with limited financial resources therefore are disadvantaged in a system that does not provide equal accessibility. Connolly et al. argue that large organizations are often supportive of eliminating network neutrality because it provides competitive business advantages and reinforces power and wealth inequality between organizations.[3]

For media organizations, the stake in network neutrality is even greater. Digital organizations that provide internet connection services (such as Comcast, Verizon or Google Fiber) stand to benefit economically from the elimination of network neutrality because it means that they can offer connectivity packages to organizations willing to pay for priority or a fast lane. Under policies of network neutrality, these Internet Service Providers (ISPs) were prohibited from granting prioritized services for pay to organizations. After eliminating network neutrality, a new revenue stream is opened to these digital organizations. It also offers possibilities of prioritizing owned content over competitor content. For example, Google could prioritize access to its own video streaming site, YouTube, and simultaneously slow down access to competitor sites like Vessel, Amazon Video Shorts or Dailymotion. In short, the elimination of network neutrality provides opportunities for greater financial and business gains.

Organizations are long identified as one of the most influential forces in public policy development on almost every issue. Large lobbying budgets, high-stakes policy decisions and resource readiness make organizations important players in the construction of policies on network neutrality. This is demonstrated in many ways, but perhaps none more than when looking at the leadership of the FCC. Nearly all FCC chairpersons appointed by US Presidents are former CEOs and business leaders, again reinforcing the closeness of organizations in the regulatory process.

Comcast was not the only organization who changed the articulation of policies after the 2017 FCC announcement. Media organizations such as Google and Facebook were similarly criticized for even small changes in policy stances which pivoted away from previous statements about aligning or appreciating a culture of network neutrality. Journalists criticized organizations who had previously vocalized support for network neutrality and suggested that they were always hiding a secret desire for the elimination of the practice. While historically this desire needed to remain secret to avert political and popular criticism, once the FCC announced intentions to eliminate the practice, this discourse slowly started to change. *Slate* summarized the differences between organizations' past stances on network neutrality and inner secret desires to repeal the policy:

> It's always been the secret. Facebook, Google, all these companies, to their credit, have said, 'Net neutrality is how we were born. It's the most important to us,' but everyone also knows that it's to some degree to their advantage to climb up the ladder and pull it up after them. They have mixed motives in this area…It's against their philosophy, but not their business interests.[4]

Organizations rely upon public opinion and public support for their success and longevity.[5] It is advantageous for an organization to outwardly support popular regulatory policies and reject unpopular ones.[6] Danis argues that public support for network neutrality motivated the largest media organizations in the world to develop and articulate pro-policy stances, even when this directly opposed business or bottom-line/profit-based success.[7] In short, while opposing network neutrality made sense for large organizations because it would intensify competition for consumer access (which larger organizations were better poised to do), media companies could not outwardly support the policy's elimination because of fears of public backlash.[8]

This tension put large organizations in a precarious, but not unfamiliar position: outward support of network neutrality and undercover support of the same policy's elimination. Jansen notes that this type of stealth communication is common for large media organizations. She reflects that the public relations branch of an organization is charged with "actively conceal(ing) its [public policy] persuasive efforts from public view whenever possible."[9] Organizations vocalize support to the public, while lobby against the policy in secret.

Historically, organizations vocalizing support while lobbying against policies is not new to global business practices. One classic example includes the American Motorcyclist Association who vocalized support for the National Highway Safety Act that required motorcyclists to wear helmets. The act was popular among concerned citizens in the 1960s. However, privately, the American Motorcyclist Association lobbied against the bill, arguing that it infringed upon consumer rights. The association even sued the federal government in an effort to block the enforcement of the act.[10] The American Motorcyclist Association actions were risky, and the public was outraged when they realized that the group only vocalized support in order to align with a popular piece of legislation.[11] After public backlash, the group refined its stance to articulate support for voluntary helmet requirements and refusal to block or protest laws that might make helmet use mandatory: "The AMA believes that adults should have the right to voluntarily decide when to wear a helmet. The AMA does not oppose laws requiring helmets for minor motorcycle operators and passengers."[12] Public support and private dissent of public policy carry a risk, particularly when these incongruent actions are identified and criticized by the public.

However, large media organizations reflecting on network neutrality did not just vocalize support; in many cases, they actively engaged the public to cultivate support for the policy (even as they lobbied against it in secret). For example, just days after the April 2017 FCC announcement of the repeal of network neutrality, Netflix spokesperson Bao-Viet

Nguyen posted on Twitter that the company planned to support the "2017 Day of Action to Save Network Neutrality" (July 17, 2017), a day of global protest against the policy's repeal.[13] Similarly, Google and Amazon pledged their support for the protest movement, asking customers and fans to participate or find a way to be involved with the protest.[14] Through social media, large organizations vocalized support for the day of action, directly responded to members of the public who asked questions about changes in network neutrality policies, and encouraged followers to find a way to become involved.

Despite audience engagement and policy promotion, journalists questioned if the communication from organizations was authentic or if it was merely an attempt to align with a popular policy and benefit from the positive public opinion of network neutrality. *The Atlantic* argued that organizations like Netflix and Google primarily supported the policy because of positive public opinion, not because of philosophical or business motivations.[15] Furthermore, although the organizations pledged support for the Day of Action, in reality, organizations did little more than tweet or blog to actually support the endeavor.[16]

Evidence suggests that organizational reactions to the 2017 FCC announcement may be a product of digital dialogic communication and the engagement of members of the audience to co-construct public policy stances. Social media platforms such as Twitter provide an opportunity for organizations to research public opinion and use it to develop strategic messages. The plethora of public support on digital media (conceptualized in Chapter 6) provides clear evidence to organizations that network neutrality was a popular policy. Thus, aligning with the policy, organizations could similarly benefit from this popularity and goodwill. Organizations like Google, Netflix and Comcast all articulated policy stances, constructed through dialogic communication, that would appeal to the public.

Problematically, their secretive or stealthy behaviors which oppositionally worked against network neutrality policy suggest that this dialogic approach was an illusion. Organizations engaged in low-risk dialogic behaviors to appear aligned with public interests and benefit from public support. Rather than a traditional dialogic approach that inclusively and authentically uses public feedback and discourse to co-construct policy stances, organizations like Comcast generated the illusion of dialogic communication without actually incorporating public interests into corporate actions.

The illusion of dialogic communication is an advancement to digital dialogic theory and seemingly extends beyond network neutrality policy development. Any organization that uses dialogic communication to build policy stances that are undermined by oppositional stealth actions engages in an illusion of the practice. And, while Comcast serves as a clear example of this illusion, many other large media organizations engaged in this practice throughout the network neutrality debate. Seven of the ten largest telecommunication organizations in the world serve as a case study for this organizational behavior. These ten companies control roughly 85% of the world's telecommunication content, including newspapers, television, internet connectivity, mobile and satellites. However, their value and widespread access is greatly dependent upon the regulatory policies that influence their size, scope and reach.

The following sections illustrate how each organization co-constructed policy stances on network neutrality using audience feedback while engaging in separate (often oppositional actions) actions to influence or shape the policy.

Comcast Corporation

Potentially the most publicized example of an organization engaging in dualistic behaviors on network neutrality is communication giant, Comcast. The multi-billion dollar global ISP provides internet connections between organizations and audiences around the world. While on the surface, Comcast vocalized support for network neutrality, including the infamous (now deleted) 2014 pledge, the company's history of suing the FCC over the constitutionality of network neutrality and demanding pay from competing organizations (such as Netflix) suggests that this was part of a pro-network neutrality illusion. As early as 2005, Comcast was investigated for deliberately showing down or blocking customer access to specific websites, thus violating key principles of equal accessibility ensured by network neutrality.[17]

One of Comcast's earliest infractions of a neutral internet occurred in 2007, when the Electronic Frontier Organization reported that the ISP "intermittently blocked access" to BitTorrent, a website with hundreds of illegally obtained music and programing files.[18] Comcast falsely blamed the blockage on network interference rather than a systematic or strategic choice to block and slow down consumer access to the site.[19] Months later, the Electronic Frontier Organization found evidence of this systematic blockage, and Comcast finally admitted that there had been no interference other than the organization's own desire to slow down access to torrent websites, a direct violation of network neutrality.[20] Perhaps motivating this blocking behavior was the competitive content of BitTorrent, a site that provided free access to popular media content (such as movies and songs) that were owned by larger media organizations. For Comcast, who owned media production companies, BitTorrent represented a challenge to its economic success. If customers had easy access to media content for free, why would they pay Comcast? While BitTorrent was far from the largest online torrent website, it seemingly represented many of the anxieties of larger organizations during the early 2000s.

Years later, Comcast again was accused of blocking and slowing down access to a media site that challenged its economic success. As reported in the introduction, Comcast was accused of slowing down access to Netflix, the largest media streaming site in the world. Comcast demanded that Netflix pay interconnection fees or an "arbitrary tax" as it was defined by Netflix CEO Reed Hastings.[21] After years of legal battles, Netflix and Comcast reached an undisclosed deal to ensure consistent service between customers and Netflix in 2014.

Also in 2014, Comcast proposed a $45 billion merger of Comcast and Time Warner Cable, potentially the largest media merger in US history. Although the deal was never approved, after months of scrutiny from members of Congress, begrudgingly, Comcast proposed a caveat to the deal, which would require the organization to uphold principles of network neutrality until 2018, even if the FCC eliminated the policy. CNET reported that once Comcast was pressured into upholding network neutrality as a part of the deal, they immediately became less interested in the proposed merger. For Comcast, a merger with Time Warner Cable would give the organization "unprecedented market power" to regulate access between organizations and customers.[22] In short, it was governmental pressure of network neutrality that killed the merger deal and Comcast's dreams of gatekeeping connection between organizations and customers.[23]

It was just about the same time that Comcast struck interconnection deals with Netflix and dropped merger plans with Time Warner Cable that they unveiled the network neutrality pledge (later deleted). The pledge promised "Comcast is committed to an open internet," and a series of five organizational commitments including "Comcast won't block access to lawful content," and "Comcast will inspire innovation, promote learning, and create access to jobs."[24] This pledge remained on the site until 2017, when the FCC announced intentions to eliminate network neutrality.

Importantly, some critics never thought Comcast's pledge was an authentic expression of support for the policy.[25] However, in the days after the FCC's decision, Comcast demonstrated just how much that pledge was disregarded by the company. First, the pledge was replaced by three statements explaining the organization's stance on the policy including "we do not block, slow down, or discriminate against lawful content" and "we believe in full transparency in our customer policy." While seemingly similar in nature to the original pledge, important discursive differences exist between the two versions. The first version uses future-oriented language such as "we will" and "won't." The later pledge uses present-voice language such as "we believe." This is a significant difference because it suggests that while the first pledge was a commitment to future endeavors, the updated pledge was a reflection on current practices and open to change in the future.

Additionally, just days after the FCC ruling, Comcast revealed a new consumer-oriented campaign designed to interpret network neutrality for everyday users. An amorphous spokesperson, "Dan," replied to hundreds of inquiring customers through Twitter to clarify the organization's stance on network neutrality. Despite this outreach effort, "Dan's" use of jargon such as Title II and "open internet" seemingly served to confuse or alienate customers further, rather than truly educate them about network neutrality provisions. Consider this scathing review from Gizmodo:

> Theoretically, it's smart strategy. Who the f*** really knows what Title II is, let alone net neutrality? Jargon like this can be useful, especially when it's used to distract consumers who don't have much expertise in arcane policy procedures. After all, most people probably don't know that Title II is the only thing that gives our current net neutrality policy any teeth. It's important to remember, however, that ISPs are also pretty clueless, particularly when it comes to convincing the public to trust them. In the clumsy hands of telecom giants whose terrible reputation precedes them, the plan of attack has turned into a chorus of lame blog posts, bizarre videos, and frantic tweets at random people on the internet. In fact, so far, the fight they've put up has been odd, uncertain, and, frankly, lame as hell.[26]

Comcast is not alone in the receipt of public backlash toward campaigns from post 2017 FCC decision. Similarly, in a series of digital videos, Verizon general legal counsel Craig Silliman was interviewed by "Jerry," an average-looking male host designed to represent customers. Throughout the interviews, Jerry asks questions such as "What is Title II" and "Does Verizon support network neutrality?" The videos are designed to give Verizon control over its own policy narrative, giving official interpretations of key provisions of the policy. And while the videos have a high production value, they were clearly rejected by the mass public. To Gizmodo, the "Jerry" campaign was just another example of the illusion of dialogic communication. Jerry and Dan represent an average customer, so giving them an opportunity to discuss network neutrality with one of the policy leaders for each organization was emblematic of Comcast and Verizon listening and engaging the public in policy decisions. However, this illusion was foiled by the organizations' history of pretending to engage in dialogic communication while simultaneously working against the exact policies the public desired.

Comcast's move away from supporting network neutrality and aligning itself with FCC decisions to eliminate the policy perhaps best illustrates how the illusion of digital dialogic works. Although for years, the organization promoted its alliance with the popular policy, the 2017 FCC decision to eliminate network neutrality provided an opportunity to finally come clean with elimination desires.[27] In short, after 2017, Comcast no longer had a use for illusion on this issue, meaning they were free to vocalize and explain why the organization opposed the policy. Comcast's communication approach pivoted from an illusion of dialogic communication to an explanation and defense of elimination network neutrality.

Walt Disney Company and 21st Century Fox Inc.

While Comcast's battles for and against network neutrality were largely public, other organizations held more tangential and quieter reflections on the policy. The Walt Disney Company was one organization with seemingly large stakes in the policy decisions which developed rapidly toward the end of 2017. After a December 2017 $52 billion deal to take control of 21st Century Fox was approved, the company now held "massive leverage over the content industry," which *The Verge* journalists argued could be used to compete with large ISPs who own their own content (such as Comcast): "Because Disney now owns so much content, other media companies have greater incentive to consolidate to improve their bargaining positions."[28] The Disney/21st Century Fox merger not only gave Disney more media power but also pushed ISPs to consolidate their own power and perhaps attempt to purchase other media content producers. This starts a chain of vertical integration, meaning ISPs attempt to integrate production into their dissemination services to take advantage of their ability to limit customer access.

The Walt Disney Company case study exemplifies a somewhat problematic part of network neutrality debates: that most customers are locked into a relationship with one or two specific ISPs. Most customers have limited choice in their ISP, and in many regions around the world, only one ISP is available. The limited ISP competition motivates content organizations to fulfill any demands from the ISP in order to maintain customer access. Content organizations that refuse to pay for internet fast lanes (or who are unable to do so) lose access to valuable customers. Thus, it is not only advantageous for ISPs to begin to acquire content organizations (to streamline this access), it is also advantageous for the content organizations.

The Boston Globe reported that a major motivation for the Disney merger included 2018 plans to start two streaming services to compete with the success of Netflix.[29] The merger allows Disney to add 21st Century Fox titles to its digital library and also control the production of future 21st Century Fox shows and films.[30] Importantly, this would also give Disney control of Hulu, another Netflix competitor with ties to ISP Comcast. *Adweek* adds that this relationship is appealing for advertisers who want to spend marketing budgets on ISP-owned streaming services "in order to guarantee a lag-free ad experience."[31]

Despite this clear strategic move as Disney positions itself within the new network neutrality free era, the organization failed to explicitly take a stance on the policy through a series of question and answer sessions hosted by CEO Bob Iger.[32] While on the surface, Iger reiterated that the company would not take an official stance, his later statements in the same session demonstrated the organization's relationship to the policy: "We've never really believed net neutrality is really an issue for us and we continue to believe that's the case, and with this acquisition, we believe that to be even more of the case."[33] His statement illustrates that the merger can impact the organization's ability to conduct business in the post-network neutrality era. While cryptic, Iger doubles down on a common vocalized discourse from The Walt Disney Company: that great content can overcome all barriers in the distribution process. Iger adds, "We believe that nothing will really stand in the way of great content, in-demand content, and the consumer."[34] Yet the company's actions suggest that this is a surface-level discourse, meaning that it does not truly represent Disney's organizational strategy or philosophy. If this discourse was correct, there would be no reason to merge with 21st Century Fox Inc. The company's competitive strategy and merger suggest that there is a larger desire to work against network neutrality and align with ISPs like Comcast who similarly oppose the policy.

While the Walt Disney Company has never explicitly taken a stance on network neutrality, they similarly take advantage of the illusion of dialogic communication. As Disney publicly reflects that network neutrality does not impact its business dealings, the organization simultaneously strategically reacts and positions itself. Although it is not as dramatic of the illusion created by Comcast, Disney's use of the question and answer sessions attempts to demonstrate and inform engagement and understanding between the public and the organization, all while the organization is already taking strategic steps against the popular policy. The illusion of digital dialogic in this case may not elicit strong public criticism, but it still fails to authentically use public feedback to inform and construct organizational action and communication. The consequences of Disney's digital dialogic illusion are yet unknown.

DIRECTV and AT&T

In July 2015, DIRECTV and AT&T completed a merger to become one of the largest ISPs and pay TV provider in the world.[35] AT&T's acquisition came after months of review by the FCC and Congress. AT&T CEO Randall Stephenson reflected, "Combining DIRECTV with AT&T is all about giving customers more choices for great video entertainment integrated with mobile and high-speed Internet service."[36] Despite this frequent statement, consumer advocate groups and publications questioned if the merger would truly hold good outcomes for customers. *Consumer Reports* wrote

> But Consumer Reports and its policy and advocacy arm, Consumers Union, don't believe that bigger companies do better for their customers. In fact, the opposite is often true. The largest companies have earned low scores for value, service, and customer satisfaction in our recent consumer surveys.

Consumer Reports alludes that promises made by DIRECTV and AT&T of better service were empty. These statements were discursively vague and provided no details of how consumers would benefit. For example, consider AT&T's official statement issued on the day of the acquisition. There were no mentions of "lower prices or better customer service, high priorities for most consumers."[37] These intentionally left out statements demonstrate that the real intentions behind the merger may be more regulatory than consumer-centric.

While it is not uncommon or wrong for an organization to merge with another for a singularly competitive business advantage, what is problematic is the use of dialogue to galvanize the public behind the illusion of support for network neutrality. As Linklater notes, dialogic communication is supposed to reflect ethical principles of transparency and a genuine attempt to integrate public feedback into policy decision-making.[38] Here, the ethical principles are violated and the dialogue is an illusion to bolster public support.

As a provision of the FCC's approval of the acquisition, Chairperson Tom Wheeler required AT&T not to prioritize DIRECTV content and to file regular reports on interconnection agreements with other content providers like Netflix.[39] *USA Today* summarized consumer advocate outrage over the additional provisions:

> Despite the promises, net neutrality proponents' howls of protest will continue for months given that AT&T's deal removes yet another competitor in the TV-Internet businesses. The increased concentration of power among the few who provide broadband Internet would give AT&T more leverage if — as the FCC has preliminarily proposed — ISPs are ultimately allowed to charge for 'fast lanes' of the Internet for content providers that are willing to pay for them.

Further, *Fortune* argues that the additional provisions on network neutrality by the FCC in the DIRECTV and AT&T deal give the combined organization a rhetorical advantage, meaning that they can argue that they uphold network neutrality to the public (because they are required to do so) while lobbying against it in private. *The Washington Post* argued that AT&T comes off looking like a proponent of the popular network neutrality policies, even as they "are prepared to fight interconnection fiercely."[40]

Just two years after the acquisition of DIRECTV, AT&T again attempted a vertical integration merger with another large media content producer, Time Warner Cable. This second merger was met with more opposition and attempts for federal blockages (including a lawsuit from the Department of Justice) potentially resulting from the organization's earlier protests of interconnection and network neutrality.

Time Warner and Time Warner Cable

Time Warner Cable was one of the first media organizations to receive a complaint for violations of network neutrality in 2015.[41] Streaming media provider Commercial Network Services (CNS) registered two complaints with the FCC for violations of the network neutrality provisions of "no paid prioritization" and "no throttling."[42] The company argued that Time Warner was deliberately slowing down access of consumers to the site and that Time Warner demanded payments from CNS to avoid congested internet traffic routes.[43] CNS alleged that Time Warner intentionally slowed down customer connections until the site paid for prioritized interconnection services. Similar to earlier violations alleged between Netflix and Comcast, Time Warner argued that CNS was not a large enough content provider to qualify for free interconnection services, thus justifying the additional fees.

CNS is a nontraditional streaming service that shares live-webcams streams to (most) customers coming from a military background. To CNS, asking for additional interconnection fees clearly violated the FCC's ruling for an open internet devoid of paid preferences. However, critics argued that the CNS case illustrated a fundamental problem with 2014 network neutrality policies: the vague nature of their enforcement. *The Washington Post* wrote,

> The agency's regulations establish hard and fast rules against slowing or blocking Web traffic, as well as a ban on content companies paying for speedier service once their traffic enters a provider's network. But by design, they don't say nearly as much about how companies should negotiate the private agreements that ensure Web traffic flows smoothly into an Internet provider's network — and to your home.[44]

This is commonly referred to as the "last mile argument," where network neutrality is regulated based on access of customers through the ISP to their desired site, not the speed of information from the organization to the ISP. The 2015 FCC Chairperson, Tom Wheeler, referenced the "last mile argument" as he dismissed CNS's complaints against Time Warner. Specifically, Time Warner operated similarly to other ISPs, allowing them to negotiate the private agreements of a content provider to the ISP.

Time Warner consistently argued that despite CNS's allegations, the ISP clearly upheld network neutrality rules and provisions.[45] And, while the ISP declined to issue an official stance on network neutrality, the organization frequently referenced operating within the constraints of network neutrality. Further, the company aligned with other organizations outspokenly against the policy such as The National Cable and Telecommunications Association, which implied that the organization similarly opposed network neutrality.[46]

A 2018 anticipated merger between Time Warner and AT&T also illustrates the close relationship between the organization and the policy. The $85 billion deal originally halted because of a 2017 lawsuit from the Department of Justice to block vertical integration that could create a monopoly (particularly without the protections of network neutrality). AT&T is one of the largest fiber-optic networks in the world and Time Warner is one of the largest ISP and content creators in the United States. A merger would give the combined organization unprecedented control over access and content distribution. *The New York Times* reported that the merger would be anticompetitive, meaning it would give dominating control to AT&T and Time Warner and prevent competitive pricing between the two organizations.[47] The anti-competition would ultimately hold ramifications for customers, who may be disadvantaged without access to AT&T. For example, AT&T could then restrict access to Time Warner programing (including CNN and HBO) if it was for noncustomers.

The provisions of eliminating network neutrality put AT&T and Time Warner in a precarious position. In order to demonstrate that the merger would not create a monopoly, they needed to advocate for the re-establishment of network neutrality or the creation of a federal network neutrality law.[48] AT&T issued full-page advertisements in major newspapers across the country in January 2018 advocating for a federal policy (as opposed to dozens of state policies) or internet bill of rights. While on the surface, these advertisements illustrate a supportive AT&T, discursively they are vague and offer no specific recommendations for network neutrality policies. David Golman of CNN (owned by Time Warner Cable) even reflected that the advertisements intentionally left questions: "AT&T may also have trouble getting consumer advocates on board. Stephenson didn't provide any specifics, including whether the bill of rights would block controversial 'fast lanes' for services and sites that pay broadband companies for preferential treatment."

AT&T's own history of regulatory fights illustrates that 2018 pro-network neutrality advertisements may by surface-only discourses. *Wired* magazine reflected that AT&T failed to learn from the history of earlier mergers with DIRECTV and underestimates the efforts of the Department of Justice to block a merger with Time Warner. *Wired* reported statements from AT&T/DIRECTV that showcased true anti-network neutrality priorities at both organizations:

> AT&T/DirecTV's own words show they aim to follow this strategy: the company says it intends to 'work to make [online video services]

less attractive.' The executives have concluded that the 'runway' for the decline of traditional pay-TV 'may be longer than some think given the economics of the space,' and that it is 'upon us to utilize our assets to extend that runway.' The merger would give AT&T increased power to do just that.

Again, as AT&T released advertisements in major newspapers across the country supporting the free and open internet, it simultaneously articulated anti-network neutrality desires in internal documents, creating only an illusion of support.

While the AT&T and Time Warner Cable merger is currently waiting for a trial (to start in March 2018), it is clear that articulated stances from the companies may not reflect inner efforts to oppose network neutrality or create paid prioritization practices.

CBS and Viacom

As one of the ten largest telecommunication organizations in the world, Viacom is relatively quiet about network neutrality. Unlike other organizations, Viacom not only refuses to take a stance on the issue, but also stayed out of lobbying efforts behind the scenes. However, the organization still holds a stake in the outcome of the 2017 network neutrality elimination. *Fortune* magazine reports that Viacom could benefit financially as a medium-sized company because it could be the target of an acquisition, similar to earlier mergers of Time Warner Cable, DIRECTV and AT&T.[49] This could cause stock market value to increase as interest in acquiring a content producer like Viacom grows. *Fortune* predicts a similar pattern for CBS.

This is not to say that these organizations want to be acquired or merged. Viacom has a history of blocking content during contract or acquisition disputes that strongly mirror network neutrality practices. For example, in 2014, Viacom suddenly blocked its content from Suddenlink customers during a contract dispute over cable broadcasting rights. This included access to Music Television (MTV), Nickelodeon and Comedy Central (and digital streaming services associated with each network). While the block primarily focused on television content and did not violate network neutrality, this practice mirrors Comcast's approach of slowing down Netflix streaming services while negotiating interconnection fees. Although it would be a leap to conclude that Viacom would engage in similar practices in a network neutrality debate, these past organizational behaviors do draw public criticism for placing profits ahead of consumer satisfaction.

Suddenlink did not quietly bow to Viacom's demands and equated the practice with violations of network neutrality. In statements issued on its affiliated websites, the organization said, "in doing this, Viacom is violating the principles of an open Internet. If you agree, please consider contacting the FCC."[50] Media researchers similarly critiqued the practice. BTIG media analyst Rich Greenfeld argued

> Importantly, CBS and Viacom disabled access to content for all ISP customers, even if those ISP subscribers did not take a video programming package...In essence, CBS and Viacom are taxing ISPs for content they make freely available on the web.[51]

Thus, while Viacom failed to take an official stance on network neutrality, its practices when negotiating with ISPs and cable providers demonstrate its oppositional perspective on the policy.

The scrutiny faced by the AT&T and Time Warner merger could perhaps challenge any possible acquisitions or mergers of Viacom or CBS particularly in an era without network neutrality. Past actions and organizational philosophies against network neutrality could potentially cause greater scrutiny and political intervention in case of a merger. As AT&T found in its attempts to acquire Time Warner, a history of nonnetwork neutral actions can motivate government blocks of major media integration, even if an illusion of pro-network neutrality exists.

Digital Dialogic Illusion

The illusion of dialogic communication is an advancement of the theory relevant to the network neutrality debate and other telecommunication organization business practices. This illusion intends to generate goodwill between the organization and the public, without assuming any of the risk associated within inviting public comment and engagement (and needing to incorporate the feedback into actions). Here, these messages use the illusion of dialogic communication to enhance public support, but fail to uphold the principles and practices of true dialogic communication.

So how do organizations create the illusion of digital dialogic practices? First, most organizations either publicly articulated support for network neutrality or appeared to endorse it as a part of merger and acquisition deals. During this process, organizations requested feedback from the public, hosted open forums or symbolically demonstrated dialogue between a public representative and organizational leader. For example, Comcast's use of "Dan" on Twitter allowed users to ask questions and receive personalized responses from the organization on the topic of network neutrality. While this may have been two-way communication, it stopped short of true dialogue and adjustment to public feedback.

Linklater's work on dialogue perhaps best conceptualizes the difference between Comcast's actions and true digital dialogic communication as thick versus thin dialogue.[52] In thick interpretation of dialogue position, the receiver (in this case the organization) must recognize the public right to be thoughtfully and respectfully consulted when creating policy that pertains to them. In the thin version, organizations have a responsibility to consult members of the public when policy decisions pertain to them, but this does not mean that the organization must advocate or accept the feedback and use it to inform its own policy stances. In short, Comcast and other telecommunication organizations in this chapter subscribed to the thin interpretation, where public feedback was garnered but not used to adjust policy stance or impact policy initiatives. While both the thick and thin versions are dialogue, only the thick interpretation is true digital dialogic communication.

Historically, the thick version carries the most support from moral and ethical philosophers like Kant and Habermas. Dialogue is fundamentally important to protect the public from unintended forms of harm. The public, through dialogue, can provide feedback that may prevent harmful policies from enactment. In the thick version of dialogue, public feedback can prevent future problems because it is taken respectfully and seriously, and thus impacts the final policy outcome. In the thin version, the organization only needs to hear the feedback, not actually use it to make policy changes. Linklater writes, "dialogic communities can frustrate the efforts of actors who are purely self-interested; ideally, participants will recognise egotistical motives and detect the lack of normative impartiality."[53] In this case, as with the American Motorcycle Association, when the public recognizes that an organization is only looking for surface-level feedback or thin dialogue, they reject the organization and advocate against the policy stance.

These illusory practices could hold a whiplash effect, meaning they propel the public to support policies like network neutrality even more strongly because of public experiences with organizations limiting access and feedback. In short, the misuse of dialogic communication holds ramifications for policy support and engagement by the public.

Because of the digital nature of this regulatory messaging, each organization pretends to use dialogic communication to impact the network neutrality debate. However, the illusion of dialogic communication appears. Although each organization uses digital media to present their views, thus providing the public with a space to react or comment (through comments sections and social media posts), public ability to do so is limited and public opinion seems relatively un-responded to. Further, members of the public and journalists criticize these public posts and messages as inauthentic and inaccurate representations of true corporate aims, goals and techniques. This journalistic treatment is the focus of the next chapter.

Notes

1 Jon Brodkin, "Comcast Deleted Net Neutrality Pledge the Same Day FCC Announced Repeal." *ArsTechnica*, November 29, 2017. https://arstechnica.com/tech-policy/2017/11/comcast-deleted-net-neutrality-pledge-the-same-day-fcc-announced-repeal/.
2 Jon Brodkin, "Comcast Quietly Drops Promise Not to Charge Tolls for Internet Fast Lanes." *ArsTechnica*, November 27, 2017. https://arstechnica.com/tech-policy/2017/11/comcast-quietly-drops-promise-not-to-charge-tolls-for-internet-fast-lanes/.
3 Michelle Connolly, Clement Lee, and Renhao Tan, "The Digital Divide and Other Economic Considerations for Network Neutrality." *Review of Industrial Organization* 50, no. 4 (2016; 2017): 1–18.
4 April Glaser and Will Oremus, "Tim Wu Explains Why Tech Companies That Love Net Neutrality Have a Ton to Gain from It's Demise." *Slate Magazine*, December 13, 2017. www.slate.com/blogs/future_tense/2017/12/13/tim_wu_explains_why_the_tech_companies_that_love_net_neutrality_have_a_ton.html.
5 Ansgar Zerfass and Muschda Sherzada, "Corporate Communications from the CEO's Perspective: How Top Executives Conceptualize and Value Strategic Communication." *Corporate Communications* 20, no. 3 (2015): 291.
6 Andrej Danis, "Network Neutrality and Ownership Unbundling in Telecommunication." *Creative and Knowledge Society* 2, no. 1 (2012): 44–59.
7 Ibid.
8 Nicholas Economides and Joacim Tåg, "Network Neutrality on the Internet: A Two-Sided Market Analysis." *Information Economics and Policy* 24, no. 2 (2012): 91–104.
9 Sue Curry Jansen, *Stealth Communication: The Spectacular Rise of Public Relations*. Cambridge: Polity, 2017: 3.
10 Adam E. M. Eltorai, "Federally Mandating Motorcycle Helmets in the United States." *US National Library of Medicine*, 2016. www.ncbi.nlm.nih.gov/pmc/articles/PMC4784405/.
11 Marian Moser Jones and Ronald Bayer, "Paternalism & Its Discontents: Motorcycle Helmet Laws, Libertarian Values, and Public Health." *US National Library of Medicine*, 2007.www.ncbi.nlm.nih.gov/pmc/articles/PMC1781413/.

12 American Motorcyclist Association, "Voluntary Helmet Use." www. americanmotorcyclist.com/About-The-AMA/voluntary-helmet-use-1.

13 Syaed Wassem, "Massive Protest against FCC Proposal to Rollback Net Neutrality." *Timely Buzz*, September 2017. www.timelybuzz.com/massive-protest-fcc-proposal-rollback-net-neutrality-amazon-google-tech-giants-participate/.

14 Jana Kasperkevic, "What Tech Companies Are Saying about the Reveal of Net Neutrality Rules." *Marketplace*, December 14, 2017. www. marketplace.org/2017/12/14/tech/fcc-net-neutrality-ruling-reaction-tech-companies-business.

15 Joe Pinsker, "Where Were Netflix and Google in the Net Neutrality Fight." *The Atlantic*, December 20, 2017. www.theatlantic.com/business/archive/2017/12/netflix-google-net-neutrality/548768/.

16 Haley Velasco, "Net Neutrality: What Happened during the July 12 Internet-Wide Day of Action Protest." *PC World*, July 14, 2017. www. pcworld.com/article/3207564/internet/net-neutrality-the-july-12-internet-wide-day-of-action-protest.html.

17 Seth Schoen, "EFF Tests Agree with AP: Comcast Is Forging Packets to Interfere with User Traffic." *EFF*, October 19, 2007. www.eff.org/deeplinks/2007/10/eff-tests-agree-ap-comcast-forging-packets-to-interfere.

18 Peter Eckersley, Fred von Lohmann, and Seth Schoen, "Packet Forgery by ISPs: A Report on the Comcast Affair." *EFF*, November 2007. www.eff.org/wp/packet-forgery-isps-report-comcast-affair#footnotes.

19 April Glaser, "Comcast Wants You to Think It Supports Net Neutrality While It Pushes for Net Neutrality to Be Destroyed." *Slate Magazine*, November 28, 2017. www.slate.com/blogs/future_tense/2017/11/28/comcast_wants_you_to_think_it_supports_net_neutrality_while_it_pushes_for.html.

20 Ibid.

21 Sam Gustin, "Netflix v. Comcast 'Net Neutrality' Spat Erupts after Traffic Deal." *Time*, March 21, 2014. http://time.com/32784/netflix-comcast-net-neutrality/.

22 Ibid.

23 Marguerite Reardon, "How Net Neutrality Helped Kill the Comcast Time Warner Cable merger." *CNet*, April 26, 2015. www.cnet.com/news/how-net-neutrality-helped-kill-the-comcast-time-warner-cable-merger/.

24 Jon Brodkin, "Comcast Deleted Net Neutrality Pledge the Same Day FCC Announced Repeal." *ArsTechnica*, November 29, 2017. https://arstechnica.com/tech-policy/2017/11/comcast-deleted-net-neutrality-pledge-the-same-day-fcc-announced-repeal/.

25 Rhett Jones, "Comcast Changed Its Net Neutrality Pledge the Day after the FCC Moved to Kill the Open Internet." *Gizmodo*, November 29, 2017. https://gizmodo.com/comcast-changed-its-net-neutrality-pledge-the-day-after-1820852207.

26 Libby Watson, "Comcast and Verizon's Sneaky Push to Kill Net Neutrality Is Just Embarrassing." *Gizmodo*, May 3, 2017. https://gizmodo.com/comcast-and-verizon-s-sneaky-push-to-kill-net-neutralit-1794846728.

27 Trey Williams, "What Netflix, Comcast and Others Are Saying about the FCC's Plan to End Net Neutrality." *Marketwatch*, November 11, 2017. www.marketwatch.com/story/what-netflix-comcast-and-others-are-saying-about-the-fccs-plan-to-end-net-neutrality-2017-11-22#false.

28 T.C. Sottek, "Net Neutrality Is Dead. It's Time to Fear Mickey Mouse." *The Verge*, December 14, 2017. www.theverge.com/2017/12/14/16776298/net-neutrality-disney-comcast-internet-providers-free-speech.

29 Hiawatha Bray, "What Net Neutrality Has to Do with the Fox-Disney Deal and Netflix." *Boston Globe*, December 14, 2017. www.bostonglobe.com/business/2017/12/14/what-net-neutrality-has-with-fox-disney-deal-and-netflix/h6Yrdsk8JvliGILw94dCCN/story.html.

30 Recode Staff, "Today's the Day for That Disney-Fox Megadeal and the FCC's Net Neutrality Vote." *Recode*, December 14, 2017. www.recode.net/2017/12/14/16774380/disney-fox-deal-acquisition-fcc-net-neutrality-vot-ajit-pai-target-shipt-apple-lasers-drew-magary.

31 Lara O'Reilly, "Unpacking the Disney Fox Deal." *The Wall Street Journal.* December 15, 2017. www.wsj.com/articles/cmo-today-unpacking-the-disney-fox-deal-net-neutrality-repealed-facebook-changes-video-strategy-again-1513342750.; Marty Swant, "Marketers Fear the FCC's Plans to Kill Net Neutrality Could Increase Advertising Prices." *Adweek*, November 22, 2017. www.adweek.com/digital/marketers-fear-the-fccs-plan-to-kill-net-neutrality-could-increase-advertising-prices/.

32 Julia Alexander, "Net Neutrality Has Never an Issue for Us, Says Disney CEO." *Polygon*, December 14, 2017. www.polygon.com/2017/12/14/16778756/net-neutrality-disney-bob-iger-statement.

33 Ibid.

34 Ibid.

35 AT&T, "About Us." *AT&T.* http://about.att.com/story/att_completes_acquisition_of_directv.html.

36 Consumer Reports Staff, "Why the AT&T-DirecTV Merger Might Actually Limit Choices for Consumers." *Consumer Reports*, July 27, 2015. www.consumerreports.org/cro/news/2015/07/at-t-directv-merger-limit-choices-consumers/index.htm.

37 Ibid.

38 Andrew Linklater, "Dialogic Politics and the Civilising Process." *Review of International Studies* 31, no. 1 (2005): 141–154.

39 Jeff John Roberts, "The FCC Just Set These Rules for AT&T's Acquisition of DirecTV." *Fortune*, July 21, 2015. http://fortune.com/2015/07/21/att-directv-conditions/.

40 Brian Fung, "AT&T Is Prepared to Abide by the New Net Neutrality Rules under the Directv Deal." *The Washington Post*, June 2, 2015. www.washingtonpost.com/news/the-switch/wp/2015/06/02/att-is-prepared-to-abide-by-the-new-net-neutrality-rules-under-the-directv-deal/?utm_term=.99cdbacfa366.

41 Mariella Moon, "Time Warner Cable Receives the First Net Neutrality Complaint." *Edgenet*, June 23, 2015. www.engadget.com/2015/06/23/time-warner-cable-faces-net-neutrality-complaint/.

42 Daniel Cooper, "TWC Is Threatened with First Net Neutrality Complaint." *Edgenet*, June 17, 2016. www.engadget.com/2015/06/17/twc-first-net-neutrality-complaint/.

43 Commercial Network Services, "Complaint Letter to FCC against TWC." *Scribid database*, June 22, 2015. www.scribd.com/document/269402621/Cns-Twc-Fcc-Complaint-Signed?ad_group=72705X1521812Xfbb74b62b13761b01 5a2ffccc0fa14fa&campaign=Skimbit%2C+Ltd.&content=10079&irgwc=1& keyword=ft750noi&medium=affiliate&source=impactradius.

44 Brian Fung, "Time Warner Cable Will Be the First to Be Hit with a Net Neutrality Complaint." *The Washington Post*, June 16, 2015. www.washingtonpost.com/news/the-switch/wp/2015/06/16/time-warner-cable-will-be-the-first-to-be-hit-with-a-net-neutrality-complaint/?utm_term=.b2d23908d2c8.
45 Ibid.
46 Todd Spangler, "Time Warner Cable Target of First Net-Neutrality Complaint." *Variety*, June 23, 2015. http://variety.com/2015/digital/news/time-warner-cable-net-neutrality-complaint-1201525929/.
47 Tim Wu, "Opinion: Why Blocking the AT&T Time Warner Merger Might Be Right." *The New York Times*, November 9, 2017. www.nytimes.com/2017/11/09/opinion/att-time-warner-merger-fcc.html.
48 David Goldman, "AT&T Wants Congress to Pass a Net Neutrality Law." *CNN*, January 24, 2018. http://money.cnn.com/2018/01/24/technology/business/att-net-neutrality/index.html.
49 Aaron Pressman, "Eliminating Net Neutrality Rules Will Favor Carriers over Internet Content Providers." *Fortune Magazine*, November 21, 2017. http://fortune.com/2017/11/21/net-neutrality-fcc-winners-losers/.
50 Todd Spangler, "Viacom Blocks Suddenlink Broadband Customers from Online Shows." *Variety*, October 1, 2014. http://variety.com/2014/digital/news/viacom-blocks-suddenlink-broadband-customers-from-online-tv-shows-1201318647/.
51 Ibid.
52 Andrew Linklater, "Dialogic Politics and the Civilising Process." *Review of International Studies* 31, no. 1 (2005): 141–154.
53 Ibid.

5 Media Interpretations

On June 11, 2018, the Federal Communications Commission (FCC) officially eliminated network neutrality policies despite ongoing Congressional attempts to stop the repeal. Journalists around the country attempted to translate and deconstruct this policy change for readers through a slew of articles with titles like "The FCC's net neutrality rules are officially repealed today. Here's what that really means." (*Washington Post*), "Network neutrality rules are dead, but the fight lives on," (*Mercury Times*) and "The Web as you know it may soon be altered as Obama-era net neutrality rules end" (*Chicago Tribune*). Headlines like these both demonstrate the efforts of journalists to translate complex policy issues like network neutrality for readers, and how they discursively construct the policy. The coverage is layered with discourses that articulate how readers should interpret the policy and engage the policymaking process. Studying these discourses provides insight into the information readers obtain when learning about network neutrality. Coverage may also demonstrate a dialogue existing between readers and journalists as they participate in the policy construction process.

Like discourses in Congressional speeches, FCC messages and organizational communication, discourses in news media help shape public understanding of political issues and policies. As one of the main ways that citizens gather information on politics and policy, the media possess an incredible potential to shape public consciousness and engagement. News media have the potential to introduce new concepts, crystallize ideas or intentions and change perspectives on contentious topics.[1] This can be particularly powerful when discourses are reinforced throughout a variety of publications or sources.[2]

In politics, media discourses are important because they hold the potential to shape political ideas, support or dissent. For citizens, news publications can break down complicated issues and demonstrate how politics are relevant for everyday life.[3] As noted, this is particularly important for topics such as network neutrality because of the complicated technical language associated with the policy.

News headlines serve a particular "discourse function" in order to "catch" the reader's attention. This means the style of discourse chosen for a headline "plays a very important part or even takes precedence over substance."[4] Allusions, for example, are a stylistic device used in headlines that Shie explains "gain audience by foregrounding a salient or interesting aspect of the news article."[5] The allusion or the double meaning of a headline refers to the primary textual meaning that includes context, and what Shie refers to as "associational meaning," or the secondary understanding that depends on association. Allusion is "an echoic reference of one unit of language in the present text (the target text) to another unit in absentia (the source text)."[6] For the purposes of this study, network neutrality, especially after 2014, is referred to in headlines as "net neutrality," likely because the style of net means more to gaining reader attention, than does the substance that network provides.

Media Coverage and Dialogic Opportunities

Although on the surface, news publications seem like spaces for one-way communication (from a journalist to a reader), there are many spaces where a dialogic communication is observed and encouraged. Historically, letters to the editor served as a space of dialogic communication when journalists published and then responded to reader inquiries. Today, engagement is found beyond letters and within news articles and the publication platforms used by journalists.[7] For example, journalists frequently shape and frame news stories in response or relationship to public issues and messages. Harcup notes that audience research is a popular way for journalists to determine what topics to cover in their next publications.[8] These suggestions come from comments sections on digital platforms as well as more traditional audience research techniques such as focus groups and interviews.[9] Journalists will often design news pieces as answers to reader questions or as if they are engaging in a conversation with an interested reader. This technique, which positions engagement as a central goal of journalism, is key in digital news coverage, particularly as journalists aim to increase reader interest and attention.

Digital spaces, such as the comments section of online news publications, provide opportunity for dialogue to take place. Participants include readers, journalists, online editors and even politicians attempting to engage the public. These spaces provide an opportunity for participants to discuss current events, share opinions and construct policy aims and goals. Comments sections are valuable because they allow members of the public to discuss journalistic coverage within the context of a news story. While this chapter looks at the dialogue that may exist within the articles themselves, the next chapter examines the comments section to look at public dialogues.

Despite previous research that identifies the possibility of dialogic communication existing within news coverage, no studies have answered the call for more research. This chapter looks at the discourses within news coverage of network neutrality in an effort to understand how the topic was discursively constructed in both popular and industry news publications. The goal is to identify the discourses that may encourage user engagement and the development of a dialogue with involved parties.

As noted in Chapter 2, public engagement in network neutrality debates was partially influenced by media coverage of the topic throughout the early 2000s. Scholars criticized both the limited attention the issue received after the 1996 Telecommunications Act and journalists' inability to make network neutrality interesting, relevant or even understandable to the general public. This was one of the reasons that Wu coined the term in the first place, since he found that the complicated language limited public knowledge and engagement in the subject. This chapter reflects on changes in media coverage of network neutrality, particularly as it highlights and encourages public engagement in the subject.

CNET, arguably one of the first online news organizations dedicated to covering internet and digital technologies, is evaluated for its longitudinal coverage of the topic. This technically oriented site, accessed by millions of users since its 1994 inception, has copiously covered network neutrality for 25 years (although it first started calling it "network neutrality" in 2000). While written for a technologically advanced audience, CNET was one of the first digital news platforms to cover issues of network neutrality. Scholars note that the platform has largely advocated for network neutrality policies, often citing the internet's history of individual rather than organizational control.

Next, the chapter examines newspapers' coverage of network neutrality since 2000 in the ten largest newspapers in the United States (*Wall Street Journal, New York Times, Chicago Tribune, New York Post, Los Angeles Times, Washington Post, Newsday, Mercury News, East Bay Times* and *Star Tribune*). It examines the techniques used by journalists to help build understanding of the topic. It also presents institutional biases in the coverage of network neutrality.

CNET Coverage

In the 25 years of coverage in CNET, network neutrality eventually emerged as a central and significant issue for the publication. Within this coverage, a series of three discourses is identified that demonstrate how the publication aimed to construct and make relevant the topic for readers. CNET is a leading industry news publication, featuring coverage of digital technology breakthroughs and its impact on daily life.

Politicization

Most articles on CNET discuss the political context of network neutrality, specifically exploring the political positioning of the policy from Republican and Democratic points of view. During each US Presidential election, CNET publishes a "Technology Voters Guide" for each candidate, outlining their stance on technological issues. In the 25-year span of CNET, each election included some reflection on network neutrality (even before the terminology was codified). These guides include quotes from interviews with the candidates. The continued inclusion of network neutrality in these political voting guides demonstrates the politicization given to the issue within the publication.

Outside of elections, CNET coverage largely demonstrates network neutrality as a democratic policy, one that is opposed by Republicans because of its implications for big business. Frequently, network neutrality is called an "Obama-era policy" suggesting that the President's Democratic leadership (not the FCC's) activated the policy. Further, CNET carefully archived Democratic Congressional members' efforts to overturn the 2017 FCC decision. Republicans, alternatively, are discursively constructed as supporting the policy's elimination in order to help large telecommunications businesses.

Within the political coverage, Republicans are also described as caring more for winning the policy debate rather than protecting consumers. CNET's selection of quotes from Republicans like Senator John Thune who calls the Democratic efforts to block the FCC's ruling, "grandstanding" and an "exercise in futility."[10] Here, network neutrality serves to entrench differences between the two parties and is more about which side wins than the creation of a policy that is in the interest of the public.

The political discourse closely mirrors the findings from Senate discussions and speeches in Chapter 2. Again, the policy itself is not innately owned by either party (especially because it is not directly regulated by elected officials), but there is a mediated effort by CNET to demonstrate it as a Democratic focus. This matches the efforts of Democratic senators as they attempted to cultivate votes to challenge the 2017 FCC ruling.

Corporations

Outside of political coverage, CNET also featured organizational network neutrality policies. Frequently, large telecommunications corporations, such as Comcast, were positioned as desiring an elimination of the policy. AT&T and Comcast were often cited as working against and pushing the boundaries of network neutrality in efforts to increase profits or audience. Within these articles, large telecommunication organizations are often positioned as putting profits ahead of ethical policies and regulations. In the aftermath of the 2017 FCC decision, CNET published an article that highlighted the tech industry's reactions to the policy elimination. Specifically, AT&T, Comcast and Verizon are highlighted as working against network neutrality policies because of the utility classification of broadband. For CNET, this classification prevented monopolistic practices.

This discourse emerged much earlier than the 2017 decision. In 2009, CNET covered a Verizon CEO statement on network neutrality, criticizing the organization's response to new regulations and misinterpretation of the policy. Through the language of "slams," the article describes how the CEO overreacted and spoke without full information on the policy.[11] Similarly, AT&T was criticized in 2009 for attempting to subvert network neutrality and play "gatekeeper" between users and digital content.[12] Again, the publication used critical language such as "playing" and "limiting" to denote the practice as outside of ethical business practices and legal regulations.

Similar to the findings of Chapter 4, CNET identified instances where organizations created an illusion that they supported network neutrality, even while they integrated non-neutral policies into business plans. A 2010 article on Google and Verizon and each organization's personal commitment to network neutrality criticized the pairings rumored business dealings which might provide ample room to negate network neutrality (even as the organizations petitioned Congress and the FCC for a stricter policy).[13] While both organizations denied the possibility of a joint venture, CNET was quick to point out that this pairing could challenge network neutrality.

Saving Network Neutrality

In the few days after the 2016 Presidential election, CNET reported on how a Republican-appointed leader of the FCC could impact policies like network neutrality. Ajit Pai, who was favored to become the new chair, was outspoken against network neutrality in his previous appointments, and thus the publication saw the policy as something that would need protection in the future. The language of "saving" was dominant throughout CNET coverage, particularly under Pai's tenure. As this term implies, the policy needed to be protected against FCC action which might hold greater implications for online conduct and the development of technology. In a 2018 piece on network neutrality advocates, the article uses words such as "battleground" and "fight" to explain how advocates are protecting the policy and attempting to save it from elimination later in 2018. This language reinforces the discourse of "saving" and constructs the current political climate as contentious.

This is also apparent in the coverage of Montana in 2018, where, through executive order, network neutrality was implemented within the state. The policy required all ISPs with state contracts to uphold network neutrality within Montana, regardless of federal action. In the CNET coverage, the state is praised for upholding and protecting the policy, rather than allowing FCC regulations to upend it. Quotes from Governor Bullock include performative language, such as "it's time to do something about it."[14] Here, CNET praises actions rather than passive support for the policy.

The language of "saving" suggests that the policy is under attack, and for CNET, it is clear who is doing the attacking: large telecommunication organizations, Republican officials and the FCC under Chairman Pai. As highlighted here, CNET positions each as the enemy of network neutrality. So who does the saving? Over 25 years, CNET developed a long list of potential individuals who protect(ed) the policy, including President Obama, Chairman Wheeler, Democratic Senators and consumer activist organizations. While far from voicing support for each, CNET implied its approval of their actions and intentions.

Newspapers

This section reflects on the challenges of making the topic of network neutrality relevant for general readership. It examines the headlines and "lexical allusions" used by journalists to help build understanding of the topic. It also presents institutional biases in the coverage of network neutrality. In the early years on the topic, especially prior to 2010, and continuing until 2014, variety from individual reporters was smaller than first imagined. This is because although all publications in the dataset included stories on the topic of network neutrality, some were reprinted/rerun headlines and stories. In the early years of coverage and reporting on network neutrality, the number of individual voices reporting on the issue was very limited. So that often the same reporter was one of a few or only voices covering the issue. This matters especially in headline news coverage, when the headline may be the only part of the story some readers are ever exposed to. In Gee's discussion of significance, the main clause of a sentence or phrase is "central" because it emphasizes the information that was intended to be the most important or prominent. The following section highlights the three discourses that were prominent in headline news coverage.

What Is Network Neutrality, Again?

The adoption of policy issues like network neutrality in popular discourses is a complex process. Research has demonstrated that members of the public are likely to adopt "technical language" on technical issues because they "feel as if they understand" the issue.[15] This discourse that represented the confusion and lack of clarity from the public, and the news media, was overwhelmingly the strongest and most common in the dataset. Many headlines throughout the span of time from 2004 to 2018 include some variation of defining "net neutrality" and indicating the likelihood that the reader and author are similarly confused. Readers are primed to be "baffled" or "confused" and the topic is often "defined" or "explained" in question form as well as declarative statement. The headlines often suggest that the topic is unwieldy, and that uncertainty over understanding is the remaining barrier to activism. This overly technical "secondary" understanding of network neutrality, unfortunately perhaps makes the issue seem more complicated than it is, which can have implications for regulation. This positioning of network neutrality as overly complicated persists throughout the dataset so that even in 2017 and 2018 when the phrase has become more likely to be included in a headline for relevance, the concept is framed as difficult to understand.

Everyday Impact of Network Neutrality

In this discourse what is made significant is the impact or direct effect the existence or removal of net neutrality will have on the everyday.

This reflects the strategy many grassroots campaigns have taken to bring awareness to the issue as well. This discourse focuses on what life will be like every day with or without net neutrality for a wide selection of the population. Most of this kind of discourse was written in a nontechnical way so that economic impact in simple terms, for example, would be emphasized rather than the technical specifics of network access. The everyday in the future tense was also framed around loss, as different outlets would explain how everyday life would lose something without net neutrality in place for many citizens.

What is also emphasized here is how much the internet has become a part of everyday life for most people, and thus the issue of net neutrality. In other words, because the internet is such an integral part of all facets of life now, most people's everyday lives would be fundamentally changed or impacted without it. This discourse was especially strong in 2014 and 2017.

Compressed Coverage

Although the issue did receive coverage from multiple publications in the dataset, headline news coverage was generally lower until 2014 and by 2017 all publications covered the issue as headline news regularly. However, prior to 2010, the same article would sometimes appear across multiple publications. This meant that the number of viewpoints and coverage in general was compressed. Several outlets would simply run the same version of a story on the topic, by the same reporter. The reportage was less varied in this way until the issue became one that was recognizable to the general public, with the numbers of all publications beginning to increase in 2014 and really exploding with "net neutrality" headlines in 2017.

Identical articles in this form of compressed coverage decrease later in the dataset, but even the first identified discourse that emphasizes explaining net neutrality reflects this sameness. This lack of variety seemed to lead to a sort of tentative discussion of the topic in news coverage that focused only on understanding what it was and why it mattered.

News Discourses and Dialogue

Newspaper headlines can be defined as "relevance optimizers"[16] that require both reporting and editorial staff to understand what their readers want to read. This means that both reporters and editors need to know what their audience generally finds relevant, and worth reading. Relevance is what is made significant.[17] Overall, it was not a headline issue for most publications in a regular way until 2014, when the issue gained real salience. 2017 and 2018 continue this trend with ever-expanding coverage and diversity of opinion. This trend certainly continues and grows as public engagement and recognition of the issue expand.

Similarly, in 2014, John Oliver's coverage of network neutrality had an impactful contribution to the meta narrative around the issue, with Oliver using humor to reframe the issue. This form of engagement between audience and performer again fulfills "the promise" of dialogic capabilities present in contemporary online civic discourse.[18] This is the focus of the next chapter. This demonstrates a dialogic turn in journalistic coverage of network neutrality and the affordances required to do so. It also reflects on how eliminating network neutrality may hinder the dialogic capabilities of shows like Oliver's or coverage like CNET's by slowing down access to content that supports network neutrality legislation.

Journalist framing network neutrality coverage as a response to reader inquiries also displays a dialogue between journalists and readers. Many pieces, such as the "what is net neutrality again?" discourses, demonstrate how journalists aim to answer reader questions and shape their coverage to fit the needs and interests of readers. Further, journalists seemingly motivate other dialogues to take place, such as the *Washington Post* articles which directed readers to contact the FCC through the commenting system or the *Mercury Times* articles which encouraged readers to share their thoughts on network neutrality in the comments sections. While the comments sections are the focus of the next chapter, it is important to note that news coverage largely motivated dialogues between other parties (not just dialogue with the journalists). In short, news coverage may have motivated dialogic communication in other spaces and with other participants, although an experimental study is necessary to confirm this motivation.

Similarities exist between newspaper coverage and CNET digital industry coverage. For example, both news sources directed readers to the FCC online commenting system, encouraged readers to discuss network neutrality with friends and family, and suggested readers join movements such as the Network Neutrality Day of Action in 2017. All publications reflected that reader and citizen engagement in the issue was necessary as the FCC decided to continue or eliminate the policy in 2017. Importantly, for news publications, engagement was seemingly synonymous with dialogue, meaning the journalists wanted readers to form a dialogue with players in the policy construction process, such as members of Congress, the FCC and organizations. Within the coverage, dialogue between readers and regulators was offered as a solution to the tensions surrounding the issue. For example, newspapers called upon the FCC to pay attention to citizen comments, and for citizens to make comments.

While it's difficult to say what impact this directly had on network neutrality policies, journalists clearly positioned dialogue between all involved parties as a central part of the network neutrality debates. Whether the dialogue took place through official channels, such as the FCC commenting system, calls to governmental representatives or inquiries to telecommunication organizations, dialogue was positioned as critical. This stance on dialogue reflects a commonality between the network neutrality coverage and other issues: dialogue is important in the policymaking process and for a healthy democracy. For example, in the discourse on saving network neutrality, journalists suggested that the best way to demonstrate outrage at the elimination of the policy was for readers to contact regulators and share interpretations and reactions. Here, the language of "saving" and "dialogue" is woven together, as if dialogue is the only path to save the policy.

It makes sense that if dialogue is centrally positioned as important to the development of policy, organizations would go to great lengths to cultivate the illusion of dialogue. While there was little coverage of the illusion of dialogic communication, from a public relations perspective, not embracing dialogue fully could be a liability and publicity risk.

The next chapter looks at comments sections and alternative journalism practices for further evidence of dialogic communication within the network neutrality debate. While most of the dialogic here is subtle, some of the discourses appearing throughout journalistic coverage appear again in the comments section, this time showing a direct relationship between media discourses and public engagement and dialogue.

Notes

1 Marjut Johansson, "Everyday Opinions in News Discussion Forums: Public Vernacular Discourse." *Discourse, Context & Media* 19, (2017): 5–12.
2 John Sonnett, "Climates of Risk: A Field Analysis of Global Climate Change in US Media Discourse, 1997–2004." *Public Understanding of Science* 19, no. 6 (2010): 698–716.
3 Bahaa G. Ghobrial and Karin G. Wilkins, "The Politics of Political Communication: Competing News Discourses of the 2011 Egyptian Protests." *International Communication Gazette* 77, no. 2 (2015): 129–150.

4 Shiung Jian Shie, "Allusions in New York Times and Times Supplement News Headlines." *Discourse and Communication* 5, no. 1 (2011): 43.
5 Ibid.
6 Ibid.
7 Rachel Davis Mersey, Edward C. Malthouse, and Bobby J. Calder, "Focusing on the Reader: Engagement Trumps Satisfaction." *Journalism & Mass Communication Quarterly* 89, no. 4 (2012): 695–709.
8 Tony Harcup, "Asking the Readers: Audience Research into Alternative Journalism." *Journalism Practice* 10, no. 6 (2016): 680.
9 Ibid.
10 Margarite Reardon, "Network Neutrality's Rescue Effort Is 'Exercise in Futility,' Says Senator John Thune." *CNET,* May 18, 2018. www.cnet.com/news/net-neutrality-rescue-effort-is-exercise-in-futility-says-senator-john-thune/.
11 Margarite Reardon, "Verizon CEO Slams Net Neutrality." *CNET,* October 21, 2009. www.cnet.com/news/verizon-ceo-slams-net-neutrality/.
12 Margarite Reardon, "Is AT&T Playing Gatekeeper to the Wireless Web?" *CNET,* June 18, 2009. www.cnet.com/news/is-at-t-playing-gatekeeper-to-the-wireless-web/.
13 Margarite Reardon and Tom Krazit, "Google, Verizon Propose Net Neutrality Framework." *CNET,* August 9, 2010. www.cnet.com/news/google-verizon-propose-net-neutrality-framework/.
14 Michelle Meyers, "Montana Becomes the First State to Implement Net Neutrality." *CNET,* January 22, 2018. www.cnet.com/news/montana-becomes-the-first-state-to-implement-net-neutrality/.
15 F.C. Robinson, "The Adoption of Technical Terms in Popular Discourse." *Sewanee Review* 119, no. 2 (2011): 308–315.
16 Daniel Dor, "On Newspaper Headlines as Relevance Optimizers." *Journal of Pragmatics* 35, no. 5 (2003): 695–721.
17 James Paul Gee, *How to Do Discourse Analysis: A Tool Kit.* New York: Routledge, 2011.
18 Craig Rood, "The Gap between Rhetorical Education and Civic Discourse." *Review of Communication* 16, no. 2–3 (2016): 135–150.

6   Public Involvement

In a June 1, 2014, episode of *Last Week Tonight*, John Oliver focused on what he described as one of the most critical issues of modern technology: network neutrality. In a 13-minute segment, titled "Network Neutrality," he described the challenges to the past and potential future of internet, and digital regulations, asserting that while the topic may be "boring," it was nonetheless important. After carefully defining the term and why the audience should care about it, Oliver concluded that there was still time for the public to engage in shaping upcoming legislation before the Federal Communications Commission (FCC) issued its final ruling on a free and open internet. Oliver addressed the "internet commenters" and asked them to message the FCC though the official commenting system, which was set up to take reactions from the public for a period of 120 days. In a concluding quote that achieved viral status online, Oliver extolled, "Turn on caps lock, and fly, my pretties!" Within hours, the FCC commenting system had crashed due to unprecedented traffic, including 45,000 posts that referenced Oliver's show. Day explains that often satire does not have an immediate, measurable effect on an audience but that instead the attention brings "incremental change" to an issue.[1] Therefore unlike much of other satirical political news, Oliver's instantaneous impact on the ongoing debate highlights the need to study the specific network neutrality context and *Last Week Tonight*.

In addition, government officials, industry leaders and other media outlets concluded that Oliver's segment had a profound effect on public opinion and knowledge of the network neutrality issue. Months later, when the FCC upheld network neutrality, Oliver's segment was again referenced throughout editorials and opinion pieces around the world as fundamentally influencing the issue's outcome. However, within these often complementary articles, questions remained regarding the status of Oliver's show, his intentions with the segment and how his larger body of work (interviews, episodes and written articles) can be conceptualized. Was Oliver a journalist who sought to inform his audience of network neutrality? Was he an advocate who intended to launch a public campaign that would influence the FCC? Was he a hybrid, a result of our current sociopolitical environment that shapes the news force? In short, how could Oliver's contribution within network neutrality be understood and placed within current mediated society? The undecided nature of these questions suggests that Oliver's work can be viewed as what other scholars have identified as alternative journalism.[2]

Oliver's network neutrality coverage highlighted the complex role of comedian-journalists, also known as "alternative" media, who have gained prominence and importance in the American political system over the past two decades.[3] In the spirit of Stewart, Colbert and countless others, the clear and measurable effect of Oliver's segment demonstrated instantaneous success and brought forward the often less visible and more longitudinal effects of these hosts.[4] Furthermore, due to the public nature of the FCC commenting system, as well as the 11,000 YouTube comments posted less than one week after Oliver's segment went viral, the emotional labor of the audience as they respond to the complicated role of the host can also be investigated.

Therefore, Oliver's use of comedy and satire in the network neutrality debate is a form of alternative journalism. The success of this alternative journalism, which in this case sought to influence public action in network neutrality debates, is dependent upon the emotional labor of the audience. This labor is often the invisible portion of the labor involved in alternative journalism, as there are few means of directly looking at cause and effect relationships between this format and audience action. However, the network neutrality segment presents a unique opportunity to study the seemingly invisible or criticized work of comedy and satire in news reporting, alternative journalism and the audience because of its heavily documented nature.

Baym notes that alternative journalism is a growing part of the global media system, one that continually gains public support and influence.[5] As a result, it is important to study a case like John Oliver to fully theorize and explore what this may mean for the future of media industries. It is also critical to the network neutrality debates that are ongoing in other parts of the world. For example, as India drew closer to a ruling on their own form of open internet, policy-makers and lobbyists struggled to build public support and interest in the issue. After examining the success of alternative journalism and Oliver in America, Indian lobbyists set out to create their own comedy routine – which was successful in building public support. It is clear that comedic alternative journalism as a practice of public advocacy is a growing trend in the network neutrality lawsuits around the world, reinforcing the need to explore it thoroughly.

Alternative Journalism and Public Advocacy

Atton describes alternative journalism as directly opposed to traditional forms that dominated newspapers and television for decades before the early 2000s.[6] He argues, "Alternative media privileges a journalism that is closely wedded to notions of social responsibility, replacing an ideology of 'objectivity' with overt advocacy and oppositional practices."[7] Thus, channeling Postman in his reflection, he argues that alternative journalism does what traditional journalism cannot: advocates, engages, entertains and still acts as a mechanism for learning. This foundational text asserts that advocacy and journalism, while once considered separate and incommensurable, today not only coexist, but are part of the normalized news experience. Journalists can do the work of advocates while not completely abandoning their roots in investigation, information and acting as public watchdogs.[8] In fact, it is the public that has seemingly demanded this transition to alternative news practices. The popularity of programs and hosts that act as journalist-advocates demonstrates the growing success and demand for this journalism format.[9]

However, understanding that alternative journalism exists and recognizing its impact and place within the American media system are two different things. While many scholars have identified the growing examples of alternative journalism, many others also recognize that alternative journalism is treated as inferior to traditional journalism, citing its newness and sense of humor as the inability to take issues and current events seriously.[10] This is frequently the way alternative journalism is treated by the mainstream or traditional media.

The public also has difficulty recognizing the role of alternative journalisms in society, although it would appear that trust of and loyalty to comedic or parodic news and alternative journalism programs are growing rapidly. Muhtaseb and Frey note that while alternative journalism was largely viewed as problematic by the public in the 1990s because it was perceived as less accurate, trustworthy and important, today, it is viewed as a fundamental part of a citizen's media diet.[11] Part of what explains this change results from the public's opinion that traditional media, particularly in the post-9/11 environment, could no longer be trusted to provide an unbiased or accurate picture of society.

Minority groups, particularly those who felt like they were unfairly represented by traditional media (i.e. Arab Americans, African Americans and young people), turned to alternative formats because they believed these might better represent their interests and needs, and act as an advocate for their audience.[12] This growth of the audience of alternative media helped it snowball and gain other audiences as well.

However, this growth in audience did not necessarily translate to gaining respect or recognition by traditional media formats. Bishop notes that alternative media struggled to gain recognition from traditional media companies and journalists, who often cited the comedy used in alternative journalism as a weakness of the format.[13] The comedy is described as distracting or pandering to the audience, which is critiqued for being too soft or lacking a critical edge.[14] Despite the growth in alternative programs and audiences, the lack of recognition and respect of alternative journalism made the format misunderstood.

However, more recent work suggests that both public and traditional media opinions of alternative journalism may be shifting, and network neutrality may be the cause of this.[15] Alternative journalism is viewed as an increasingly relevant and valid means to describing critical issues that were once deemed too boring or esoteric for public interest. Being able to describe issues like network neutrality in a means that is understandable and relatable, and entertaining to the general public is described as an asset by those who usually criticize this format. Delli Carpini notes that "scholars starting from very different places are converging on the observation that entertainment matters to politics."[16]

It was out of this type of critique of television journalism and media that *The Daily Show* grew into what Baym calls "alternative journalism."[17] Baym identified that although the conversation in the media often focused on the apathy of the younger generation toward political engagement, young people were tuning in to late-night comedy television to get their news, a trend that has continued since his article was first published ten years ago.[18] Although late-night comedy had poked fun at the politics of the day for decades, Baym found that *The Daily Show* was contributing something that was not only new to the genre but an almost entirely new instance genre of comedy and news, "alternative journalism."[19]

It is important to note, however, that Jon Stewart and his producers insisted on calling their program "fake news" (not "alternative journalism") and refused to apply the label of journalism to their product. The label of journalism has been applied to the program by Baym, and scholars since then, but the host and producers of Stewart's version of the show have always remained adamant that what they do is comedy and "fake" news, not journalism.[20]

Baym found the label of "fake" problematic for several reasons. One of his main criticisms stemmed from his recognition that any version of "fake" necessitated a version of "real" to exist as the opposite.[21] He wrote: "Fake news necessitates assumptions about some kind of authentic or legitimate set of news practices, ideals that one rarely hears articulated or necessarily sees as evident today."[22] The show took the form of "discursive integration" by blending genres, formats and a "way of speaking about, understanding, and acting within the world defined by the permeability of form and the fluidity of content."[23] For example, Stewart's participation in an interview with Ron Paul functions as a "hybrid mode of speech," that constructs Stewart as something different than a regular journalist: a citizen. This hybrid form of talking allows Stewart to ask questions in a way that is difficult if not impossible for someone who occupies the job of a traditional journalist, because he is not constrained by the same set of norms and rules.

Political Satire and Public Engagement

Recently, political scholars have defined the role that satire plays in the political process. Hill employed a critical approach and positioned satire as a kind of "counter-narrative" to create a normative approach for studying political satire.[24] This approach questions if it was possible for satire to influence beliefs, and whether or not that influence was good for democracy. This emphasizes a focus beyond the material a comedian or satirist employs but also especially on the boundaries created by the genre of satire as a narrative form.[25]

One of the boundaries created by the form of satire is the notion of taking a position. A journalist is constrained by different rules and norms than a satirist when reporting on an issue, and is therefore meant to remain objective while simply reporting what has or will occur. A satirist must do nearly the opposite and take a position to tell the story they wish to tell. Hill writes that "it is this set constellation of positions that produces a sense of normality between individuals and social institutions that satirists attempt to disrupt and distort."[26] This is important because by taking a position, the satirist can create a "counter-narrative" that aims to distort and highlight that which is normally taken for granted. Institutional truths that have become normalized over time are positioned as ridiculous by a satirist, and they offer resistance to traditional political discourses.[27]

The work of satire again is rarely instant as changes generally occur in incremental shifts.[28] Viewers tune in to "watch the real be critiqued and transformed."[29] Larger societal and cultural transformations emerge from satire, with the help of audience engagement. Recent effects' studies on political satire have highlighted this issue. In her study of Colbert, Day found that he "greatly magnified public discussion," both on campaign finance and the current system in use.[30] Although there was not an immediate measurable change, Colbert, in his comedic persona, raised the public conscious on an issue that might otherwise have gone unnoticed.

Wrapped in issues of identity within the scope of alternative journalism are the changing roles of audience and engagement. If alternative journalism assumes that the journalist can go beyond informing the audience and instead ask them to engage in an issue, this engagement is held in the balance.[31] Gibbons writes that "if it is accepted that dialogue between the holders of different values is desirable—or even necessary for a democratic society to persist, some effort should be made to persuade citizens to engage with one another."[32] Audience engagement with an issue is thus the goal of instances of alternative journalism, as demonstrated by Oliver's request for commenters to message the FCC. This is a central difference in the conceptualization of alternative journalism from traditional forms. Previously, traditional hosts asked the viewer to engage with the television show, while today's alternative journalist asks the audience to leave the show and engage with an outside organization, topic or campaign.[33] In short, it is the conceptualization of engagement that has shifted in the alternative journalist format.[34]

So how can the engagement of alternative journalism be studied? As mentioned by Delli Carpini's work, measuring this new form is difficult because of the entrenched nature of theorizing engagement that primarily studies how the audience engages with a message, not necessarily the actions taken after.[35] However, this study contends that audience engagement in alternative journalism can be studied by examining immediate audience reactions. Like other media formats, the audience is of central importance in alternative media programs like *Last Week Tonight*. If shows like this are understood as alternative journalism, then the audiences' reactions to the messages, influence strategies and formatting are a fundamental part of the success of the shows. Barnes notes that studying engagement in alternative journalism must examine the feedback of the audience to the host/program as well as the actions adopted toward the outside organization or issue.[36] Harcup agrees and terms it two-directional engagement, a type of active citizenry that demonstrates both media literacy and political/civic participation.[37]

In an effort to study this two-directional engagement, scholars have taken to reading message boards, social media content and online databases where the audience writes messages to the show, host or producer.[38] If the goal of these programs is to both inform and persuade, research into the audience's reaction may help make visible the often opaque and fuzzy boundaries of alternative media and traditional journalism. By inquiring into the audience's opinion of Oliver's segment, particularly how it understands his goals, his use of comedy and the effectiveness of his delivery, it is possible to address some of the invisible qualities and engagement of alternative media.

By engaging his audience through satire, and being ridiculous himself, Oliver pointed out the ridiculous that is intrinsic to government itself. And in showing his viewers how and what to do, he "made visible" what an engaged public could actually do about this issue if it bothered them. By using comedy in this more discursive way, a host of an alternative journalism program could create a dialogue with their audience rather than a monologue.

Oliver, HBO and Format-Fragmented Media

While the audience of alternative news programs has undergone tremendous changes in the past two decades (including race, gender and age demographic changes), so have the venues and distribution strategies of these shows. While *Saturday Night Live* was one of the first television shows to attempt a comedic take on the news, Comedy Central became one of the first networks to embrace a comedic alternative news format, and HBO has also hosted several shows noted for pushing the boundaries of comedy and journalism. In the summer of 2014, Oliver premiered his new show *Last Week Tonight* on the HBO network, continuing in the tradition of what Jon Stewart and *The Daily Show* call fake news, alternative journalism.

The show is similar in format to *The Daily Show*, with strong elements of parody, engagement and studio interviews, but differs from the "Daily News Segment" portion of the programming for several reasons: (1) *Last Week Tonight* is only once a week in a half-hour format, so it cannot truly emulate or mimic the "daily" format; (2) instead of only emulating and simultaneously mocking the "now this" mentality of traditional news the way *The Daily Show* does to great comedic effect, Oliver also conducts what he calls "deep dives." So, while the show is divided up into segments, the bulk or meat of each episode is devoted to one topic so that in format, Oliver's program bears a much closer resemblance to a news program like *60 Minutes* than it does to the nightly news or *The Daily Show*.

On June 1, 2014, Oliver aired the fifth episode of *Last Week Tonight*, titled "Network Neutrality" and employed one of his shows "deep dives" on the topic of network neutrality. Oliver explained the situation and highlighted how deeply "boring" the traditional news media coverage was on the topic, commenting that it was not surprising how many people didn't understand or care about the issue. He in fact made the case that this boredom was something that those opposed to network neutrality were counting on, because a disengaged public might not notice how important the issue was until it was too late to get involved.

The segment lasted 13 minutes and ended with Oliver speaking directly to his audience, asking them to participate by commenting on the FCC's website. "Turn on caps lock, and fly my pretties!" he yelled at the end of the program, and fly they did. By Monday, June 2, the FCC's commenting system no longer worked, thanks to over 45,000 comments received since Oliver's show aired, inspiring many online think pieces about the efficacy of Oliver's approach: "'We all agreed that John Oliver's brilliant network neutrality segment explained a very complex policy issue in a simple, compelling way that had a wider reach than many expensive advocacy campaigns,' the spokesman, Nu Wexler, said."[39] Part of that wider reach included those who viewed the video on YouTube, and many of those viewers also left comments.

Past research has identified studying YouTube comments on viral video content as a means of understanding momentary and immediate reactions of the public to media content.[40] Rather than waiting for a researcher to interview an audience subject, or changing medium in diary entries, YouTube comments are viewed as a reliable means of identifying the discourses, nuances and narratives of immediate audience reactions.[41] Additionally, Havens, Lotz and Tinic note the methodological contribution of D'Acci's influential work to the critical approach utilized here.[42] D'Acci performed an in-depth analysis of letters from the audience of *Cagney and Lacey* to the network, which demonstrated that specific "representations resonated in the realm of people's lived experiences."[43] D'Acci stressed that the importance of audience responses, even on a small or case scale, is as important as the study of institutional structures in general.[44]

Comedy

When examining the YouTube comments, it is clear that comedy is the primary mechanism for drawing in the audience and encouraging them to participate in Oliver's request for FCC commenting. Comedy is what makes Oliver's introduction and analysis of network neutrality interesting, helpful and different than other forms of media coverage. For example, users commented that Oliver's video is what made them "understand" what neutrality was, and many commented that his video was "hilarious."

For the most part, Oliver's use of comedy is applauded because it helps the audience understand a complex issue. Important here is that the audience acknowledges that they did have an interest in network neutrality before Oliver's segment, but it was not until they watched it that they felt like they understood it. This is critical as it is not Oliver who introduces the topic to the audience, but he is the one who makes it relatable through the alternative journalism format. Comedic alternative journalism, then, is the tool used to make the topic interesting, approachable and relevant to the audience. Building upon this analysis, many posters also encouraged others to watch the segment, hoping that it may bring them insight too, emphasizing that Oliver's take would help them to "understand."

Like earlier posters, here the audience engages in sharing behavior, using the affordances of Google+ and YouTube to share it with their own followers. Of the over 11,000 posts on the segment, there are 5,430 users who posted that they had shared it with their connections on Google+ accounts. While it is impossible to know how many additional views this sharing behavior generated, it is clear that the audience's work to engage others by suggesting the video on their Google+ pages was important to the success and distribution of Oliver's coverage of the network neutrality debate.

Similarly, the sharing behavior almost always denoted a type of appreciation of his coverage and use of comedy. In these instances, the commenters described his comedy using terms such as "brilliant" and "necessary."

Comedy is what makes Oliver's coverage unique and especially insightful. It is again separated from other forms of media and deemed more legitimate than the coverage generated by traditional sources and legislative proponents. This separation reinforces the "alternative" quality of alternative media, in that it recognizes the void left in the coverage of policy by traditional formats.

Alternative Journalism

There is continued evidence that the audience recognizes Oliver and his show as existing outside of the traditional media landscape. Many posters congratulate Oliver on his segment and the courage, energy and vision he exhibited throughout his show. After the FCC issued its network neutrality ruling, there were posts of congratulations, gratitude and appreciation, with comments of "thanks" and "thank you" and posts directly addressed to Oliver complimenting his work.

These commenters reflected that Oliver's segment was a force of good in the news industry and the American political system. They viewed his work as singularly or mostly responsible for the network neutrality victory. This is an important element of alternative journalism, as often there are few reflections in the aftermath of a political issue that directly relate a segment to the success or failure of a political agenda. Here, through the online affordances of YouTube, the audience and public could reflect on what they viewed as critical to the ongoing issue. This is also important because it recognizes alternative journalism as a crucial impetus for generating civic and public involvement, which the commenters viewed as important to the political outcome. Oliver's contribution was discursively framed as "important" and integral to the success of network neutrality, and the FCC was directly referenced often in opposition to Oliver's work.

The commenters added that they viewed the FCC's decision as related to the involvement of the public, which resulted from Oliver's show. While the FCC does state that they are open to receiving public comment, there was little policy evidence that the FCC actually takes public opinion into consideration. So it was then Oliver's show that provided the framework for encouraging public engagement in the issue, and feelings of collective victory when their demands for an open internet were upheld. There is also a view that the YouTube system encourages interaction and engagement between the host and its audience. Many commenters added personal notes to Oliver, addressing him rather than HBO, the larger show, or production team. By addressing their comments to Oliver directly, there is a sense that his show builds engagement and action, rather than a passive relationship.

Engagement

In addition to noting that they shared the video on Google+, many commenters added that they were inspired by the segment to contribute to the FCC Commenting System. In addition to appreciating and applauding his comedy, the audience added what steps they had taken to hopefully engage and influence the outcome of the network neutrality debate. Many commenters expressed the idea that they did not usually or typically publicly comment on most things online, but that Oliver's segment had "inspired" them. The term "inspired" appeared throughout these posts, indicating the plan to take action or engage.

There were also instances where the commenters engaged with each other, asking them to take specific steps or echoing Oliver's encouragement to contact the FCC. Many commenters responded to each other, especially on comments where they asked who else had written to the FCC. This also happened frequently during the first two months of the FCC Commenting System being open for public comments on network neutrality when the system crashed because of the high traffic.

Dialogue

How can YouTube comments use digital dialogic communication to engage the network neutrality debate? While an unconventional space, YouTube provides a similar platform for user engagement and dialogue. Historically, digital dialogic research has examined social media platforms, organizational websites and message forums. However, YouTube serves as a space where users can post responses to specific videos that act as a catapult for conversation and discussion. Additionally, YouTube comments contain feedback, the same feedback that is critical for the formation of public policies that can be analyzed by journalists, politicians and organizational strategists. Even simple retweets, shares or likes on YouTube provide some cursory information for organizations who elicit feedback.[45]

Veenstra et al. argue that YouTube comments are rich areas of public feedback and information for organizations because of their location on a third-party website.[46] Participants posting feedback on YouTube videos are liberated from concerns of retaliation or deletion by content owners or organizations. This produces more depth and emotional content from users when compared to posts on official organizational platforms or accounts. And Oliver's segment is not the only video that elicited digital responses on network neutrality. "Network neutrality in the shower" was a viral video where John Green, also known as the "VlogBrothers," explained network neutrality while showering. The video similarly elicited responses to network neutrality and the humor used to explain the policy. Similarly, Chairman Pai's videos which sarcastically describe how daily life will (or will not) be impacted by network neutrality draw public comment and responses.

Further, research demonstrates that YouTube comments are regularly attended to by public relations counselors and media monitors. YouTube is now a space that should be monitored for public feedback and reactions, as is the case in political campaigns.[47] While it has taken years for public relations practitioners to develop a technique to effectively collect and analyze comments, research shows that some organizations are using YouTube comments to identify and engage specific opinion leaders.[48] John Oliver's network neutrality segment highlights how these comments are interpreted by organizations and media representatives. Oliver directly quoted a series of comments from previous YouTube videos to illustrate the trolling behavior he sought for the FCC commenting system.

While it is unclear if telecommunication organizations used the public feedback from Oliver's segments in their policy development, journalists readily did so when analyzing the success of the Oliver's call for FCC comments. *Slate, The New York Times* and *Fortune* all directly quoted YouTube comments in celebrations of Oliver's work, demonstrating that a relationship existed between users and journalists through YouTube. Although journalists did not reach out or respond to all users, their reinforcement and use of quotes from YouTube in articles and news coverage demonstrate that some communication and adjustment took place.

Further, mutual adjustment is identified when examining how journalistic coverage evolved following the impact of Oliver's segment. While previous journalistic coverage reflected on a disengaged and apathetic public toward network neutrality policy, Oliver's segment and the massive number of FCC comments forced journalists to recognize newfound public involvement on the issue. The unprecedented number of YouTube and FCC comments demonstrated the large number of interested citizens, thus requiring journalists to adjust or evolve coverage to reflect this involvement.

The dialogic communication style between journalists and citizens appears elsewhere in the network neutrality debate. Numerous articles from CNet, *Time* and *The Wall Street Journal* draw upon audience questions posted within chatrooms and on commenting systems. Tech Republic even ranked the most frequent questions from citizens about network neutrality, using these questions to drive and design articles and videos explaining key concepts and components of the policy.[49]

Further, politicians and political representatives seemingly also used public comments to frame and design information on network neutrality. In 2014, Advisor for Senior Advisor for Technology and Economic Policy David Edelman used Reddit to participate in an "ask-me-anything" forum where users could ask questions about network neutrality.[50] Here, Edelman drew from citizen posts on Reddit and YouTube videos to frame his conversation and responses. The American Civil Liberties Union participated in a similar ask-me-anything session in 2017, again demonstrating the efforts of advocacy groups to engage and use dialogic practices.

In short, nearly all parties except large telecommunication organizations demonstrated use of YouTube comments when developing policy stances and communicating positions on network neutrality. This is not to say that organizations did not take notice. In fact, it is likely that organizations used information garnered from these sites in a more private way. Organizations clearly tried to publicly align with network neutrality policies, even when they secretly lobby against network neutrality. It is likely that the public support on YouTube and other forums was a motivating force for this illusion of support. These spaces may have provided the primary public opinion data that motivated organizations to feign support of the policy.

YouTube, like most other digital media platforms, is globally accessible to citizens around the world. This means that national association is impossible to reliably identify. The digital space blurs national boundaries and allows individuals from any background to comment or participate in the digital dialogic. While it is likely that most of the posts on Oliver's YouTube video were American, the success of his clip was identified by International advocacy groups, such as those in India, who also sought to use digital dialogic communication to impact policy decision within the country. Global initiatives, such as those in India, Great Britain and China on network neutrality, are the focus of the next chapter.

Notes

1 Amber Day, "Shifting the Conversation: Colbert's Super PAC and the Measurement of Satirical Efficacy." *International Journal of Communication* 7, no. 1 (2013): 414–429.
2 Chris Atton, "What Is 'Alternative' Journalism?" *Journalism* 4, no. 3 (2003): 267–272; Renee Barnes, "The 'Ecology of Participation': A Study of Audience Engagement on Alternative Journalism Websites." *Digital Journalism* 2, no. 4. (2014): 542–557. doi:10.1080/21670811.2013.859863; Geoffrey Baym, "The Daily Show: Discursive Integration and the Reinvention of Political Journalism." *Political Communication* 22, no. 3 (2005): 259–276.
3 Ibid.
4 Amber Day, "Shifting the Conversation: Colbert's Super PAC and the Measurement of Satirical Efficacy." *International Journal of Communication* 7, no. 1 (2013): 414–429.
5 Geoffrey Baym, "The Daily Show: Discursive Integration and the Reinvention of Political Journalism." *Political Communication* 22, no. 3 (2005): 259–276.
6 Chris Atton, "What Is 'Alternative' Journalism?" *Journalism* 4, no. 3 (2003): 267–272.
7 Ibid, p. 267.

8 Tony Harcup, "Alternative Journalism as Active Citizenship." *Journalism* 12, no. 1 (2011): 15–31.
9 Cole C. Campbell, "Journalism and Public Knowledge." *National Civic Review* 93, no. 3 (2004): 3–10.
10 Ibid; Thomas Gibbons, "Active Pluralism: Dialogue and Engagement as Basic Media Policy Principles." *International Journal of Communication* 9, no. 1 (2015): 1382–1399.
11 Ahlam Muhtaseb and Lawrence R. Frey, "Arab Americans' Motives for Using the Internet as a Functional Media Alternative and Their Perceptions of U.S. Public Opinion." *Journal of Computer-Mediated Communication* 13, no. 3 (2008): 618–657.
12 Jill A. Edy and Shawn M. Snidow, "Making News Necessary: How Journalism Resists Alternative Media's Challenge." *Journal of Communication* 61, no. 5 (2011): 816–834.
13 Ronald Bishop, "The Accidental Journalist: Shifting Professional Boundaries in the Wake of Leonardo DiCaprio's Interview with Former President Clinton." *Journalism Studies* 5, no. 1 (2004): 31–43.
14 Ibid; Jill A. Edy and Shawn M. Snidow, "Making News Necessary: How Journalism Resists Alternative Media's Challenge." *Journal of Communication* 61, no. 5 (2011): 816–834.
15 Chris Atton, "What Is 'Alternative' Journalism?" *Journalism* 4, no. 3 (2003): 267–272.
16 Michael X. Delli Carpini, "Breaking Boundaries: Can We Bridge the Quantitative Versus Qualitative Divide through the Study of Entertainment and Politics?" *International Journal of Communication* 7, no. 1 (2013): 531–551.
17 Geoffrey Baym, "The Daily Show: Discursive Integration and the Reinvention of Political Journalism." *Political Communication* 22, no. 3 (2005): 259–276.
18 Jeffrey Gottfried and Monica Anderson, "For Some, the Satirical 'Colbert Report' Is a Trusted Source of Political News." *Pew Research*, December 12, 2014. www.pewresearch.org/fact-tank/2014/12/12/for-some-the-satiric-colbert-report-is-a-trusted-source-of-political-news/.
19 Geoffrey Baym, "The Daily Show: Discursive Integration and the Reinvention of Political Journalism." *Political Communication* 22, no. 3 (2005): 259–276.
20 Ibid.
21 Ibid.
22 Ibid, p. 261.
23 Ibid, p. 262.
24 Megan R. Hill, "Developing a Normative Approach to Political Satire: A Critical Perspective." *International Journal of Communication* 7, no. 1 (2013): 322.
25 Ibid.
26 Ibid.
27 Ibid.
28 Amber Day, "Shifting the Conversation: Colbert's Super PAC and the Measurement of Satirical Efficacy." *International Journal of Communication* 7, no. 1 (2013): 414–429.
29 Ibid.

30 Ibid.
31 Graeme Turner, "Millennial Journalism." *Journalism* 10, no. 3 (2009): 390–392.
32 Thomas Gibbons, "Active Pluralism: Dialogue and Engagement as Basic Media Policy Principles." *International Journal of Communication* 9, no. 1 (2015): 1389.
33 Ella McPherson, "Advocacy Organizations' Evaluation of Social Media Information for NGO Journalism: The Evidence and Engagement Models." *American Behavioral Scientist* 59, no. 1 (2015): 124–148.
34 Brian Martin Murphy, "Alternative 'Journalisms,' Social Movement Computer Networks and Africa." *Critical Arts* 13, no. 2 (1999): 1–23; Luke Goode, "Social News, Citizen Journalism and Democracy." *New Media & Society* 11, no. 8 (2009): 1287–1305.
35 Michael X. Delli Carpini, "Breaking Boundaries: Can We Bridge the Quantitative Versus Qualitative Divide through the Study of Entertainment and Politics?" *International Journal of Communication* 7, no. 1 (2013): 531–551.
36 Renee Barnes, "The 'Ecology of Participation': A Study of Audience Engagement on Alternative Journalism Websites." *Digital Journalism* 2, no. 4. (2014): 542–557. doi:10.1080/21670811.2013.859863.
37 Tony Harcup, "Alternative Journalism as Active Citizenship." *Journalism* 12, no. 1 (2011): 15–31.
38 Renee Barnes, "The 'Ecology of Participation': A Study of Audience Engagement on Alternative Journalism Websites." *Digital Journalism* 2, no. 4. (2014): 542–557. doi:10.1080/21670811.2013.859863; B. van der Haak, M. Parks, and M. Castells, "The Future of Journalism: Networked Journalism." *International Journal of Communication* 6, (2012): 2923–2938.
39 Ben Brody, "How John Oliver Transformed the Net Neutrality Debate Once and for All." *Bloomberg Politics*, February 26, 2015. www.bloomberg. com/politics/articles/2015-02-26/how-john-oliver-transformed-the-net-neutrality-debate-once-and-for-all.
40 Mike Thelwall, Pardeep Sud, and Farida Vis, "Commenting on YouTube Videos: From Guatemalan Rock to El Big Bang." *Journal of the American Society for Information Science and Technology* 63, no. 3 (2012): 616–629.
41 Aaron Hess, "Resistance Up in Smoke: Analyzing the Limitations of Deliberation on YouTube." *Critical Studies in Media Communication* 26, no. 5 (2009): 411–434; J. Uldam and Thomas Askanius, "Online Civic Cultures: Debating Climate Change Activism on YouTube." *International Journal of Communication* 7, (2013): 1185–1204.
42 Timothy Havens, Amanda D. Lotz, and Serra Tinic, "Critical Media Industry Studies: A Research Approach." *Communication, Culture, and Critique* 2, no. 2 (2009): 234–253; Julie D'Acci, *Defining Women: Television and the Case of Cagney and Lacey.* Chapel Hill: The University of North Carolina Press, 1994.
43 Timothy Havens, Amanda D. Lotz, and Serra Tinic, "Critical Media Industry Studies: A Research Approach." *Communication, Culture, and Critique* 2, no. 2 (2009): 243.
44 Julie D'Acci, *Defining Women: Television and the Case of Cagney and Lacey.* Chapel Hill: The University of North Carolina Press, 1994.

45 Young-shin Lim and Roselyn J. Lee-Won, "When Retweets Persuade: The Persuasive Effects of Dialogic Retweeting and the Role of Social Presence in Organizations' Twitter-Based Communication." *Telematics and Informatics* 34, no. 5 (2017; 2016): 422–433.
46 Aaron S. Veenstra, Chang Sup Park, Benjamin A. Lyons, Cheeyoun Stephanie Kang, and Narayanan Iyer, "Intramedium Interaction and the Third-Person Effect: How Partisans Respond to YouTube Ads and Comments." *Cyberpsychology, Behavior, and Social Networking* 18, no. 7 (2015): 46–410.
47 K. Hazel Kwon and Anatoliy Gruzd, "Is Offensive Commenting Contagious Online? Examining Public Vs Interpersonal Swearing in Response to Donald Trump's YouTube Campaign Videos." *Internet Research* 27, no. 4 (2017): 991.
48 Elaheh Momeni, Bernhard Haslhofer, Ke Tao, and Geert-Jan Houben, "Sifting Useful Comments from Flickr Commons and YouTube." *International Journal on Digital Libraries* 16, no. 2 (2015): 161–179.
49 Scott Mateson, "How to Answer 10 Common Net Neutrality Questions from Users and Executives." *Tech Republic*, February 16, 2018. www.techrepublic.com/article/how-to-answer-10-common-net-neutrality-questions-from-users-and-executives/.
50 David Edelman, "Ask-Me-Anything." *Reddit*, 2014. www.reddit.com/r/IAmA/comments/2lvly9/i_am_r_david_edelman_president_obama_just/.

7 Global Reach

Scientific American reports that the 2017 decision to reject network neutrality in the United States caused the country to fall behind other developed country's consumer protection regulations.[1] The magazine argued that US policies would now be similar to Brazil, famous for deregulating internet service providers and allowing telecommunication organizations to prioritize data based on network capacity.[2] Comparisons to other countries are common within debates over network neutrality, symbolizing the growing global nature of policy decisions on internet communication.[3] For individuals with looming anxiety about how the 2017 Federal Communications Commission (FCC) decision to eliminate network neutrality would impact daily life, turning to foreign regions seems to provide insights and varying levels of comfort. As a medium that allows global communication, many scholars have reflected on the irony of regulating internet using physical regional boundaries.[4] Nonetheless, as governments move toward implementing pro- or anti-network neutrality policies, the constitutive process of regulation remains dynamic across the world. Reflecting on four regions, this chapter outlines how digital dialogic communication is used globally to influence network neutrality policies.

India

Recent Indian rulings on network neutrality visualize and embody the constructive nature of public policy as developing from a number of stakeholders including the public, organizations, political leaders and regulatory offices. Since 2015, India has imposed network neutrality legislation upon all telecommunication service providers within the country. BBC News called India's regulations the strongest in the world because of the focus on core issues and direct responses to organizations that violate the order.[5] In addition, a penalty of up to Rs 50 lakh ($77,621 USD) can be imposed by the regulatory office.

In January 2017, Indian government officials announced that they would henceforth formally bar telecommunication service providers for charging additional fees to access digital content.[6] The decision came after months of public debate and earlier lawsuits against organizations from demanding payment for access to digital platforms. Similar to the 2015 FCC decision, the Telecom Regulatory Authority of India (TRAI) requested public comments through an online system for months in advance, following the distribution of the written proposed policy titled: "Regulatory framework for over-the-top services." As members of TRAI appeared on talk shows and in public forums, over one million comments were submitted to the online system, largely in favor of enacting formalized network neutrality policies.

The policy debate ignited in 2014, when large telecommunication service provider Airtel Zero announced that it would increase connection fees for users who access or communicate via Skype and WhatsApp. While Airtel defended the increased fees by citing the immense amount of data and energy required by each site, users were outraged by the climbing service fees. Similarly, Facebook announced plans to create a service called, "Facebook Free Basics" which would provide free internet access to millions of sites for free, but charge for what it deemed as "high capacity websites." This service package is popularly known as "zero rating" or "toll free data." TRAI opposed and banned these plans, citing violations of network neutrality, a policy that was never formalized by Indian Government. TRAI then published a research paper explaining network neutrality and invited citizen engagement in the topic via public forums and the online commenting system. Less than a year later, TRAI formalized its policy, citing public support during the response period.[7] Indian newspaper *LiveMint* reflected that the policy was formalized only after TRAI engaged stakeholders and sought feedback: "The decision was made after a series of consultations with stakeholders."[8] In short, the policy was co-constructed by TRAI, organizations, members of the public and other political bodies.

TRAI chairman RS Sharma reflected,

> The overarching thought that we had was for a country like India, internet is an extremely important platform. (The) internet today is a great platform for innovation, startups, banking, and government applications such as health, telemedicine, education, and agriculture. It is going to become further important in view of the

Internet of Things and a huge number of applications...Therefore, it is important that this platform be kept open and free and not cannibalised.[9]

The timing of TRAI's announcement was suspected by journalists who saw it as a direct criticism of changes in US policy on network neutrality. In a section called "big daddy US rethink," *The Times of India* reported,

> Tuesday's Trai papers came at a rather crucial time after nearly two years of deliberations, just after the US regulator Federal Communications Commission (FCC) said that it plans to roll back the net neutrality rules that were adopted in US in 2015. This will go to a vote next month. Regulators across the world take cues from its American counterpart.[10]

However, after the FCC officially approved the US reversal of policy, India remained committed to network neutrality in its own country. Activists such as Nikhil Pahwa even cited the US policy reversal as motivation for their own involvement in India's policymaking process. "The debate ... that this ruling was about was essentially the same one that's taking place in the US, about whether certain sites should be available at faster speeds."[11] Similar to the United States', TRAI's policy needs further approval from federal governmental before application; however, public sentiment seems to support keeping network neutrality.

India's ruling is relevant to other global discussions of internet regulation. India is the second largest internet and mobile market in the world (after China), with room to grow even larger since only 27% of the Indian population is connected to the internet.[12] The large population size has pushed many western telecommunication organizations to establish offices within the country, including Facebook who vocalized disappointment that network neutrality would block it's Free Basics plan: "While disappointed with the outcome, we will continue our efforts to eliminate barriers and give the unconnected an easier path to the internet and the opportunities it brings."[13]

Great Britain and EU

As a collective, the European Union institutes policies for all members on network neutrality, although some countries such as the Netherlands and Slovenia have instituted stronger initiatives on the topic.[14]

One of the first formalized reflections on network neutrality in the EU developed in 2007, when the European Commission articulated the five directives of digital content (created in 2002). While the group did not formally institute a policy of network neutrality at the time, the commission did comment on the role of prioritization in digital access: it "is generally considered to be beneficial for the market so long as users have choice to access the transmission capabilities and the services they want."[15] In this vein, the commission viewed access as a priority of upcoming legislation, although the group recognized the limitations of its current ability to enforce policies of network neutrality in a continuingly global society.

In 2009, the commission recognized the "Telecoms Package" or a policy that would require service providers uphold transparency standards when engaging in prioritization practices. This large-scale reform required telecommunication organizations to "inform subscribers of any change to conditions limiting access to and/or use of services and applications, where such conditions are permitted under national law in accordance with Community law."[16] In other words, if a telecommunication organization was going to violate network neutrality, they had to do it in a transparent way. For telecommunication organization, this transparency mandate was the foci of millions of dollars in lobbying efforts.[17] The Telecoms Package also created an international governing office, Body of European Regulators for Electronic Communications (BEREC), who would oversee communication between the regulating authorities of each EU country.

Emerging from the Telecoms Package was a sense of urgency in the EU to propose and review large-scale digital policies that would impact all members.[18] In 2015, the EU adopted a "digital single market," defined by the EU as

> one in which the free movement of persons, services and capital is ensured and where the individuals and businesses can seamlessly access and exercise online activities under conditions of fair competition, and a high level of consumer and personal data protection, irrespective of their nationality or place of residence.[19]

The three pillars of this policy include access, environment, and economy and security, and are the foundation of all network neutrality policies in the EU. In short, the "digital single market" ensured network neutrality throughout all member countries. In a statement on the European Commission's official website, the policies of a digital single market are woven through the digital single-market initiative:

It enshrines the principle of net neutrality: internet traffic shall be treated without discrimination, blocking, throttling or prioritisation. At the same time, the EU net neutrality rules allow reasonable traffic management and, with the necessary safeguards, 'specialised services'; those are services which assure a specific quality level, required for instance for connected cars or certain 5G applications.[20]

Since 2015, network neutrality policies (with limits) are required in EU member countries.

However, there is criticism that the policy's limits may create larger loopholes than intended by regulators. In a *Reuters* interview, Eduardo Santos, director of the D3 Association for the Defense of Digital Rights in Portugal, reflected: "In practice, providers are allowed to use their position as gatekeepers to favor certain services, which is detrimental to consumers, competition and innovation as far as new, smaller players are concerned."[21] Some providers are starting to split access into packages, such as a social package that offers special rates for social media sites like Facebook and Instagram. While this complies with the EU's laws, it clearly violates the principle of network neutrality. New access packages like these have motivated consumer activist organizations to protest ISPs who violate network neutrality. Marco Pierani, a spokesman for Italian consumer group Altroconsumo, reflected, "It is a battle we continue to fight ... Leaving the choice to the service providers creates a false market and places the choice in the hands of very few operators who are very strong."[22]

As with network neutrality coverage in India, the EU's policies are contrasted with US changes in policy. *The New York Times* reflected that the loopholes in the EU policy may foreshadow how the 2017 decision to eliminate network neutrality rules will impact the United States.[23] While the EU ruling created a patchwork of policies across the continent, overall, these loopholes motivated consumer activist groups to mobilize and work to enforce network neutrality in instances of question: "This a battle for the next century," said Klaus Müller, the chairman of the Federation of German Consumer Organisations, a lobbying group. "We can either have oligarchical markets with huge players, or a big variety of companies with lots of competition, which would be good for consumers but bad for big business."[24]

Australia

Australia remains one of the few developed countries in the world without formalized national laws and policies on network neutrality.

Queensland University of Technology Professor Matthew Rimmer explained, "We don't have a public interest concept of net neutrality, but nonetheless there has been a lot of concern about broadband services in Australia, particularly slow broadband speeds."[25] This means that there are frequent examples where internet service providers give different rates for access to different sites. And, while on the surface this appears to prioritize delivery of specific sites to audiences, even regulators are not clear if this is a violation of network neutrality. Vint Cerf, one of the pioneers of the internet claimed that "traffic management is not a net neutrality issue, so long as providers are consistent in their treatment of like services." In Australia, paid versus free access is a regular occurrence, and consumers view this access difference as a normal experience of digital technology.[26]

For Rimmer, although national government was slow to move on network neutrality policy (which opened the door for non-neutral practices), consumer advocates and Australian organizations were deeply involved with the issue. Critically, Australian journalists argue that the time for network neutrality policy has passed in Australia, and digital organizations are already too adapt at the paid prioritization structure to redevelop access policies now.[27] However, this does not mean that current trends in Australian access will foreshadow the United States in a post-network neutrality era. There are two major differences that have diminished the impact of paid prioritization on everyday Australian life. First, there is significantly more competition between internet service providers in Australia than there are in the United States. Unlike the United States, most Australians have a choice between internet service providers, meaning that the providers must compete to provide the best service and rates for customers. In the United States, most customers have just one choice of ISP, meaning they are subject to the rates enforced within that area. Second, Australia has strong consumer protection laws which are enforced by the Australian Competition and Consumer Commission (ACCC). This group of national regulating authorities is considered one of the leading consumer advocate groups in the world because of its strict punishment of anticompetitive initiatives.[28]

However, the global nature of the internet means that Australians could be impacted by the 2017 FCC decision to eliminate network neutrality. Although Australia did not have a formalized policy of network neutrality, many global organizations, with outputs in Australia, used the US standard as its operating procedure. This means that the US laws provided a standard that many Australian organizations upheld, even though there was no formal policy enforcing network neutrality.

Tim Singleton-Norton, a spokesperson from Digital Rights Watch (an internet advocacy group), reflected,

> With that now gone, we're worried about what Australian operators will see as an opportunity to change that…In fact, we've already seen some comments, such as from the CEO of Vodafone Australia, that he is willing to look into this as to how he could change processes here in Australia.

While the ACCC said it would keep keenly aware of any anti-competition policies emerging in Australia after the 2017 FCC ruling, consumer groups recognized the limits to the ACCC's power without a formalized policy of network neutrality.

China

Unlike the United States, Australia, India and the EU, China controls and owns the ISP's operating within its borders. In addition to other forms of digital control, China adopted the "Computer Information Network and Internet Security, Protection, and Management Regulations" in 1997, which limited the content allowed in digital spaces.[29] Reporters without Borders notes that violators of the 1997 policies are fined or imprisoned, again reinforcing the governmental control over access. In an editorial from the *New York Times* titled "What if you couldn't see this page?" the newspaper argued that China's version of network neutrality was large-scale censorship and a digital Great Wall.[30] China's practices hinder access to global websites, such as the *New York Times*, which is a violation of free speech initiatives within the United States. The editorial warns that eliminating network neutrality could produce a similar effect in the United States, where ISPs would control the information and sites available to users.

Beyond free speech implications, there are also concerns that the elimination of network neutrality in the United States could insight a trade war with Chinese and other foreign companies (or governments).[31] These international companies, with large amounts of capital, may be impacted in two ways. First, they could be invited to bid for audience access, meaning they could pay for prioritization similar to other organizations.[32] Because these international organizations have more financial capital to give, they could outbid smaller organizations and gain prioritization. Second, they could be outright blocked by specific ISPs. Benjamin Cavender, a senior analyst at the Shanghai-based China Market Research Group, reflected,

I can also see this happening that they (Chinese Internet firms) just get completely blocked because of the U.S. using this more as a trade tool trying to get more access to the Chinese market because if you are a U.S. technology company you are working at a great disadvantage in the Chinese market. I do see this being used as a trade tool.[33]

In short, the global ramifications of the FCC decision in 2017 could reach even tightly controlled countries like China.

For some scholars, China's history of controlling digital access could be a precursor to future global organizational and governmental behaviors. A vice president of the Center for Strategic and International Studies in Washington reflected, "When you look at Europeans talking about blocking each other's content, when you look at the U.S. talking about blocking Russian political warfare, the Internet cannot be the wild west that it's been for a couple of decades. So, everyone's moving in this direction and I guess the Chinese can take comfort from that."

Notes

1 Sascha Meinrath and Nathalia Foditsch, "With FCC Net Neutrality Ruling, the US Could Lose Its Lead in Online Consumer Protection." *Scientific American*, December 14, 2017. www.scientificamerican.com/article/with-fcc-net-neutrality-ruling-the-u-s-could-lose-its-lead-in-online-consumer-protection/.
2 Ibid.
3 Vlad Savov, "The US Net Neutrality Fight Affects the Whole World." *The Verge*, November 23, 2017. www.theverge.com/2017/11/23/16693840/net-neutrality-us-fcc-global-effect.
4 Andreas Fischer-Lescano, "Struggles for a Global Internet Constitution: Protecting Global Communication Structures against Surveillance Measures." *Global Constitutionalism* 5, no. 2 (2016): 145–172.
5 Prasanto K. Roy, "India Net Neutrality Rules May Be World's Strongest." *BBC News*, November 30, 2017. www.bbc.com/news/world-asia-india-42162979.
6 BT Online, "Timeline: How the Net Neutrality Debate Opened Up in India." *Business Today*, November 28, 2017. www.businesstoday.in/current/economy-politics/timeline-how-the-net-neutrality-debate-opened-up-in-india/story/264908.html.
7 Abhijit Ahaskar, "Why Trai Is Backing Net Neutrality and How It Will Affect Users." *Live Mint*, November 29, 2017. www.livemint.com/Technology/rWh2oMqvXBCtuQmFl8lBlM/Why-Trai-is-backing-net-neutrality-and-how-it-will-affect-IS.html.
8 Ibid.
9 Ananya Bhattacharya, "Net Neutrality: India's Trai Is Upholding an Open Internet as the FCC Moves to Dismantle It in the US." *Quartz*, November 29, 2017. https://qz.com/1140558/net-neutrality-indias-trai-is-upholding-an-open-internet-as-the-fcc-moves-to-dismantle-it-in-the-us/.

10 Ramarko Sengupta, "Net Neutrality: All You Wanted to Know but Were Afraid to Ask." *Times of India*, November 30, 2017. https://timesofindia. indiatimes.com/business/india-business/net-neutrality-all-you-wanted-to-know-but-were-afraid-to-ask/articleshow/61863693.cms.

11 The World Staff, "US Moves to Dismantle Net Neutrality Rules, India Moving Opposite Direction." *PRI World*, December 5, 2017. www.pri. org/stories/2017-12-05/us-moves-dismantle-net-neutrality-rules-india-moving-opposite-direction.

12 Michael Safi, "India Communications Regulator Endorses Net Neutrality Telecom Internet." *The Guardian*, November 29, 2017. www.theguardian. com/technology/2017/nov/29/india-communications-regulator-endorses-net-neutrality-telecom-internet.

13 Yuthika Bhargava, "TRAI Rules in Favour of Net Neutrality." *The Hindu*, February 8, 2016. www.thehindu.com/sci-tech/technology/internet/TRAI-rules-in-favour-of-Net-neutrality/article14068029.ece.

14 George Christou and Seamus Simpson, "Shaping the Global Communications Milieu: The EU's Influence on Internet and Telecommunications Governance." *Comparative European Politics* 12, no. 1 (2014): 54–75.

15 European Commission (13 November 2007), "Impact Assessment on the Proposals to Amend the European Regulatory Framework (Working Document – SEC(2007) 1472)" (PDF), p. 91.

16 Directive 2009/136/EC Universal services directive, see Article 20, point 1(b) second bullet.

17 Monica Horten, "Where Copyright Enforcement and Net Neutrality Collide." *Digital Commons*, 2010. http://digitalcommons.wcl.american.edu/cgi/viewcontent.cgi?article=1017&context=research.

18 Saleem Bhatti, "Net Neutrality May Be Dead in the US, but Europe Is Still Strongly Committed to Open Internet Access." *The Conversation*, January 5, 2018. http://theconversation.com/net-neutrality-may-be-dead-in-the-us-but-europe-is-still-strongly-committed-to-open-internet-access-89521.

19 European Commission, "Shaping the Digital Single Market." https://ec. europa.eu/digital-single-market/en/policies/shaping-digital-single-market.

20 European Commission, "Open Internet." https://ec.europa.eu/digital-single-market/en/open-internet-net-neutrality.

21 Andrei Khalip and Agnieszka Flak, "False Paradise? EU Is No Haven of Net Neutrality Critics Say." *Reuters*, December 15, 2017. www.reuters. com/article/us-usa-internet-eu-analysis/false-paradise-eu-is-no-haven-of-net-neutrality-say-critics-idUSKBN1E92SC.

22 Ibid.

23 Liz Alderman and Amie Tsang, "Net Neutrality's Holes in Europe May Offer Peek at Future in US." *The New York Times*, December 10, 2017. www.nytimes.com/2017/12/10/business/net-neutrality-europe-fcc.html.

24 Ibid.

25 ABC Newsnet, "Net Neutrality: The Digital Landscape Set to Change as the US Moves to Overturn Regulations." *ABC newsnet*, November 22, 2017. www. abc.net.au/news/2017-11-22/net-neutrality-regulations-to-be-overturned-in-the-us/9179512.

26 Karl Schaffarczyk, "Australia's Net Neutrality Lesson for the US." *The Conversation*, January 28, 2014. https://theconversation.com/australias-net-neutrality-lesson-for-the-us-22245.

27 Ibid.

28 Helen Davidson, "Consumer Watchdog May Investigate If Facebook Data Illegally Used in Australian Elections." *The Guardian*, March 20, 2018. www.theguardian.com/uk-news/2018/mar/20/consumer-watchdog-may-investigate-if-facebook-data-illegally-used-in-australian-elections.

29 Tom Balek, "China Has Net Neutrality: Government Control of Internet Coming to America Too." *The Watchdog*, February 23, 2015. www.watchdog.org/opinion/china-has-net-neutrality-government-control-of-internet-coming-to/article_e65d2e8f-4f77-5000-8ac1-59267b21b27f.html.

30 Nick Frisch, "What If You Couldn't See This Page." *The New York Times*, December 14, 2017. www.nytimes.com/2017/12/14/opinion/net-neutrality-china-internet.html.

31 Saibal Dasgupta, "US Net Neutrality Move May Lead to Trade War with Chinese Internet Firms." *VOA News*, January 16, 2018. www.voanews.com/a/net-neutrality-repeal-may-affect-china/4209599.html.

32 Alibaba, "Net Neutrality May Shape the Next Episode of China's Internet War." *Technode*, December 28, 2017. https://technode.com/2017/12/28/china-unicom-net-neutrality/.

33 Saibal Dasgupta, "US Net Neutrality Move May Lead to Trade War with Chinese Internet Firms." *VOA News*, January 16, 2018. www.voanews.com/a/net-neutrality-repeal-may-affect-china/4209599.html.

8 Digital Dialogic Implications

In 2016, a group of digital activists unveiled a campaign designed to engage and activate millions of global users in the fight to uphold network neutrality.[1] Through a letter-writing campaign, Battle for the Net called upon citizens to write Congressional representatives to voice support for network neutrality. The group would later create and popularize the "Day of Action to save Net Neutrality," which took place on July 12, 2017. The decentralized group, who calls themselves, "Team Internet," used digital channels to reach millions of users, including social media accounts on Facebook, Twitter and YouTube and a boldly designed website which included a "write Congress" form.

Battle for the Net was largely a byproduct of another internet activist organization, "Fight for the Future," which began in 2011 to fight against the Stop Online Piracy Act (SOPA) and PROTECT IP Act (PIPA). The nonprofit's "about us" section on the website highlights some of the groups history of cultivating online protest movements and addressing digital issues surrounding privacy and the first amendment right to freedom of speech. However, within this description are also references to dialogic communication, which are at the core of Fight for the Future's actions and campaigns.

In Fight for the Future's own words, the organization relies upon digital dialogic communication to engage the public, organizations and regulators in the network neutrality debate. Through letters to Congress, online strikes of organizations that supported SOPA and PIPA, and Federal Communications Commission (FCC) comments, Fight for the Future believes that digital dialogic communication has and can impact regulatory behaviors through patterns of mutual adjustment. Fight for the Future asks users to digitally demonstrate their support of network neutrality through a variety of communication channels, which (because of the amount) puts pressures on representatives to adjust behaviors and policies to fit the needs of the public.

Fight for the Future rests on the notion of mutual adjustment based on public demands. For this nonprofit, digital activism is the pathway to impact the network neutrality debate and policies.

Network neutrality is far from the only policy where activist organizations have called upon the public to use digital communication to attempt to form a dialogue with governmental representatives and regulators.[2] Perhaps the earliest example from 1990 focused on Lotus Marketplace, a digital database of consumer information. Posting on popular message boards, Larry Seiler, a computer professional, asked readers to contact Lotus to remove their information from the database.[3] In the end, nearly 30,000 users called Lotus, causing the organization to drastically change its privacy standards and issue an apology for the accessibility of user data.[4]

In many ways, the internet hallmarks a period of mutual adjustment because it provides a way for individuals, activists and organizations to galvanize, activate and engage users, and direct their actions toward targets. For Fight for the Future, these targets included regulators, other nonprofit organizations and even President Barack Obama. By the end of 2015, the group claimed victory and posted a "How We Won" webpage highlighting the outputs and outcomes of their campaign. Highlights included four million FCC posts, over 20 million Facebook posts, 101 civil rights groups who joined the fight and ten days occupying the FCC lawn in Washington, D.C.[5] However, it is unclear if these actions produced obvious measurable results, or were the clear catalyst for the 2015 FCC decision to classify ISPs under Title II and thus protect network neutrality. The implications are further murky considering the dismantling of network neutrality just two years later. It raises questions over the purpose and execution of digital dialogic communication, such as "is digital dialogic communication simply a system of communication or does it require the outcome of mutual adjustment?" or "how can mutual adjustment be identified in cases where regulatory outcomes contradict public demands?"

The network neutrality debate is unique because it is both shaped by digital dialogic communication and holds the potential to impact future digital dialogic communication practices. Organizations, such as Fight for the Future, were quick to draw upon digital communication because of experiences with previous issues (such as SOPA and PIPA) that demonstrated its success. However, the implications of the issue of network neutrality were even larger considering that a dismissal of network neutrality could prevent it from being used in the future.

Much of the previous research on digital dialogic communication has focused on the internet's potential to provide a space for digital dialogic communication to take place. In these examples, the focus is on organizations who seek out the input and feedback from key stakeholders, such as members of the public, to adjust organizational behavior and actions. For these organizations, the benefits of digital dialogic communication are obvious: understanding public opinion helps the organization adjust behaviors ethically and meet public needs and desires.[6] For some scholars, this is a normative assumption of 21st century life, that public feedback and engagement are helpful and desirable for competitive advantages and progress. Habermas's public sphere emphasizes the notion of public engagement through discussion for future decision-making.[7] Dialogue is considered one of the most ethical approaches to communication, and as Kent and Taylor note, "one of the central means of separating truth from falsehood."[8] While this text agrees with this normative assumption, it is worth noting that there are scholars who disagree with the involvement of the public, particularly in regulatory policy debates.[9]

Dialogic communication is directly opposite from monologic policies, or policies where an organization simply uses a digital space to direct messages outward from the organization to target audiences. In monologic communication, rather than looking for feedback or input from the public, the organization uses one-way communication and fails to utilize the full communicative potential of the internet. Instead, digital dialogic communication is a system where organizations engage the public and garner feedback to make adjustments to behavior and tactics. In Taylor and Kent's seminal article on digital dialogic communication, the system is iconized by five principles: mutuality, propinquity, empathy, risk and commitment.[10] If an organization uses digital dialogic communication and effectively upholds all five principles, it is likely that mutual adjustment, or the integration of the discussion into organizational action, will take place. However, as noted within this study of network neutrality, there were many cases where the dialogue did not result in mutual adjustment, perhaps because it was not true dialogue.

A variety of groups sought to use digital dialogic communication throughout the network neutrality debate. The FCC sought public comments on the issue in 2015 and again in 2017, large telecommunication companies used social media to discuss the issue with customers, regulators hosted virtual and physical town hall meetings with constituents and activist organizations requested that users contact governmental representatives. Each case demonstrates a desire for dialogue to take place through digital media. However, this desire was not always obvious or authentic. In many cases, after seeking feedback through digital dialogic communication, organizations performed contrary actions to public input. Perhaps the clearest example was the 2017 FCC decision to dismantle network neutrality, despite a clear majority of public comments within the FCC commenting system supporting the policy. However, the rejection of network neutrality does not necessarily mean that digital dialogic communication did not take place. In his speech announcing the decision, FCC Chairman Ajit Pai even cited the overwhelming number of comments that the commission received during the commenting period. And, although the commission did not respond to every comment, it did follow up with any policy-related (as opposed to opinion-related) posts.

This embodies a clear implication of digital dialogic communication on network neutrality: digital dialogic communication does not always result in the organization adopting the publicly supported action. Mutual adjustment can and did take place in more subtle ways. For example, telecommunication organizations joined the "Day of Action" and tweeted support for pro-net neutrality actions; Congressional representatives rejected the FCC's 2017 decision, citing public reactions as support for their own proposed legislation; and journalists published articles responding to citizen questions and inquiries.

It is also worth noting that there was a group, albeit smaller, who used digital dialogic communication to support the repeal of network neutrality in 2017. Using similar channels, this group voiced demands for the policy's repeal using the FCC commenting system, social media and requests to journalists. The Center for Individual Freedom, a conservative digital activist group that rivals Fight for the Future, took credit for encouraging members to participate in the fight against network neutrality. Although this group was smaller in size, it is possible that mutual adjustment took place using this feedback, rather than the feedback of pro-network neutrality stakeholders.

Thus, digital dialogic communication and mutual adjustment are not to be confused with acting upon the majority's opinions. Successful digital dialogic communication took place throughout the network neutrality debates, despite the FCC decision to reject network neutrality, a policy decision that most Americans (and global citizens) opposed.[11] For example, members of Congress used twitter to engage constituents about their feelings on network neutrality. Although this communication embodied all five dialogic principles, it did not mean that this communication was the only factor in what shaped a representative's opinion on the policy. Other factors, including lobbying efforts, similarly impacted opinions.

This is not to say that all moments were authentic attempts at digital dialogic communication. There were cases where organizations and individuals sought to give the illusion that they used digital dialogic communication, despite clearly rejecting and failing to integrate any public feedback into decision-making (see Chapter 4). It is easy to see why some individuals might attempt to feign an illusion of digital dialogic communication: if public involvement is considered a normative or preferable practice in policymaking, individuals tasked with creating policy aim to demonstrate some attempt at a dialogue (even when they have no interest in the outcomes of such discussion). Previous scholarship notes that reputation is positively correlated with dialogic practices on social media.[12] The public demand and expectation of mutual adjustment are likely what motivated large telecommunication organizations such as Comcast to attempt to elicit public feedback (even if they later rejected it). FCC Chairman Pai's attempts to engage and respond to Twitter users (only if to make fun of them and participate in the e-banter).

The illusion of digital dialogic communication, or what some scholars call inauthentic engagement, appeared throughout debates over network neutrality.[13] This illusion violates one of the core principles of dialogic communication, that of "empathy" and "supportiveness." Within this principle lies the intention that "participants demonstrate the 'capacity to listen without anticipating, inferring, competing, refuting, or warping meanings into pre-conceived interpretations.'"[14] Clearly, examples such as FCC Chairman Ajit Pai reject this principle by failing to listen to public feedback and rather reject and belittle public feedback through satirical YouTube videos.

Risk may be the element that prevents these organizations and individuals from truly embodying dialogic systems of communication. Public feedback can be unwieldy and produce unanticipated responses, such as protest and the expression of negative sentiments. The illusion of dialogic communication is more attractive because it separates the risk of the dialogic from the reward. It allows individuals and organizations to pretend to elicit feedback (thus appearing to align with public interests) while failing to change or adapt to integrate the unpredictable public sentiment. In short, these organizations appear to align with public interests, but instead continue organization policies and actions unencumbered or changed by public feedback.

Browning notes that the illusion of dialogic communication may inhibit the ethical potential of dialogue because it focuses on communication as an ends-based utilitarian principle where "the ends justify the means."[15] Rather than focusing on dialogue as the outcome, the policy or public opinion of the organization/individual is the focus. The ends-based approach violates the ethical and moral integrity of dialogue by shifting the priority away from mutual understanding to a singularly beneficial outcome. This illusion has seemingly motivated scholarly attention to the quality of dialogic communication and the development of a quality scale that identifies some platforms as superior in encouraging dialogic communication.[16] It is possible for two-way communication to take place without dialogue, which is at the core of the illusion of dialogic communication. Organizations aim to appear as if they use dialogue, while in reality, the discussions and conversations through digital platforms fail to truly impact decisions and policy orientations.

The differentiation of ends-based utilitarianism is emblematic of ongoing debates in public relations over the equation of dialogue and two-way communication. Paquette et al. argue that this false equivalency perhaps stifles the development of dialogic theories of public relations.[17] In this case, it is likely that many of the instances of engagement between various stakeholders and policymakers are more emblematic of two-way communication than a true dialogue. The fact that communication takes place does not mean that dialogue takes place. Dialogue is part of an "ongoing activity intended to genuinely involve the participants," not merely the presence of communication.[18]

This illusion reflects a lack of commitment to dialogue, and instead an attempt to manipulate public perception and opinion. Rather than embody the two-way, symmetrical communication styles that hallmark the communicative potential of the internet, the illusion reflects one-way manipulative or asymmetrical communication. Importantly, the repeal of network neutrality will only further inhibit dialogic communication practices online. There are three ways that digital dialogic communication can be impacted by a repeal of network neutrality. First, paid prioritization may artificially accelerate access to sites that support ISP interests or policies, while slowing down access to sites that advocate against these interests. Second, access to spaces of digital dialogic communication, such as Yelp and social media platforms, may be slowed down to favor digital dialogic spaces that are controlled by ISPs or allied organizations. Third, nonprofit activist organizations with limited capital may not be able to pay for prioritized access, thus slowing down accessibility to these sites.

Slow Down Public Comments to Generate False Support or Dissent

An immediate implication of the repeal of network neutrality is that ISPs can now regulate what sites' users can access based upon paid prioritization and the financial relationship of the ISP to the site. This gives the ISP control over what content is easily and quickly accessible, and what content is slower to load by individuals. This means that ISPs can slow down sites that it does not want the public to access, while speeding up sites that it wants easily accessible. Sites, such as Battleforthenet.com, which advocate against ISP interests would likely face higher interconnection fees and become less accessible (i.e. slower) to the public. Sites such as the Center for Individual Freedom, which aligned itself with ISPs against network neutrality, could become more easily accessible (i.e. faster).[19]

While this practice is far from being actualized at this time, the potential for the prioritization of sites that align with ISP interests and slowing of sites that dissent from ISPs is a potential in the aftermath of the repeal of network neutrality. Many ISPs have even vocalized their rejection of this practice and intentions to keep using network neutrality, even after the repeal. However, the potential remains and holds clear ramifications for those who use digital dialogic communication to impact public policy and advocacy.

Slowing down some sites and prioritizing others could falsely demonstrate the popularity of one view over another and make dissenting positions difficult to find. In short, it could falsely demonstrate the popularity of support for ISP-backed issues and make it difficult to find dissenting positions. Users attempting to find information on topics could also be directed toward ISP-supportive websites because of their prioritization, while dissenting websites are hidden or more difficult to access. As a result, gaining information or joining movements against ISP-backed policies or issues could become more difficult.

Hinder Digital Dialogic Communication

Next, access to spaces where digital dialogic communication takes place could also become more difficult under a repeal of network neutrality. This goes beyond activist websites, such as Battleforthenet. com and into sites such as Yelp, or social media platforms where organizations engage the public for feedback. These sites and platforms grow increasingly popular, meaning they take up more bandwidth and are a likely a target for increased interconnection fees. Should these ISP-demanded fees become contested, access to each platform could be slowed down. Organizations which rely upon these platforms to perform digital dialogic communication could find difficulty in their attempts to access and engage the public.

Further, ISPs could accelerate access to their own platforms or sites, thus causing public relations practitioners to rethink where digital dialogic communication takes place and the best routes to accessing members of the public.

Stifle Activist Groups

Finally, ISPs could slow down access to sites like Battleforthenet.com that encourage members of the public to partake in digital dialogic communication. Sites like this provide easily accessible ways for the public to identify and contact Congressional representatives (through digital forms on the site). In order to stifle this outreach, these sites could become slower and more difficult to access. Other barriers for contact could also emerge, such as increasing interconnection fees for nonprofit organizations around critical Congressional voting deadlines (when citizen outreach is most important). If digital dialogic communication is perceived as a threat for IPS interests, sites that encourage its enactment could become less accessible.

Sommerfeldt et al. argue that activist websites already struggle to fully engage the public and uphold the dialogic promise of the internet.[20] It is likely that this struggle will continue once faced with increasing interconnection fees and barriers in user access.

As organizations continue to use the internet to build relationships and influence policy decisions, attention to the implications of network neutrality repeal is vital to anticipating changes to dialogic systems. These systems rely upon user access, and any efforts to slow down or inhibit the connection between users and organizations may hold serious implications for activist-public relationships and impact. As policy changes continue to evolve globally, more scholarly attention to this issue is vital.

Notes

1 Roslyn Layton, "Fact and Fiction in 'Battle for the Net.'" *Forbes*, May 13, 2016. www.forbes.com/sites/roslynlayton/2016/05/13/fact-and-fiction-in-battle-for-the-net/#71ed5cfd1ac5.

2 Joohan Kim and Eun Joo Kim, "Theorizing Dialogic Deliberation: Everyday Political Talk as Communicative Action and Dialogue." *Communication Theory* 18, no. 1 (2008): 51–70.

3 Mary J. Clunan, "The Lessons of Locust Marketplace: Implications for Consumer Privacy in the 1990's." *Computer Professionals for Social Responsibility*, 1991. http://cpsr.org/prevsite/conferences/cfp91/culnan.html/.

4 Laura J. Gurak, *Persuasion and Privacy in Cyberspace: The Online Protests over Lotus MarketPlace and the Clipper Chip*. New Haven, CT: Yale University Press, 1997.
5 Battle for the Net, "How We Won." 2015. www.battleforthenet.com/how-we-won/.
6 Andrew Linklater, "Dialogic Politics and the Civilising Process." *Review of International Studies* 31, no. 1 (2005): 141–154.
7 Ibid.
8 Michael L. Kent and Maureen Taylor, "Toward a Dialogic Theory of Public Relations." *Public Relations Review* 28, no. 1 (2002): 21–37.
9 Yoo, Christopher S. The Dynamic Internet: How Technology, Users, and Businesses are Transforming the Network. Washington, D.C.: AEI Press, 2012.
10 Ibid.
11 Paul Hiltin, Kenneth Olmstead, and Skye Toor. "Public Comments to the FCC about Net Neutrality Contain Many Inaccuracies and Duplicates." *Pew Research Center*, November 29, 2017. www.pewinternet.org/2017/11/29/public-comments-to-the-federal-communications-commission-about-net-neutrality-contain-many-inaccuracies-and-duplicates/.
12 Yoo Jung Hong, Donghee Shin, and Jang Hyun Kim, "High/low Reputation Companies' Dialogic Communication Activities and Semantic Networks on Facebook: A Comparative Study." *Technological Forecasting and Social Change* 110, (2016): 78–92.
13 Jan Bebbington, Judy Brown, Bob Frame, and Ian Thomson, "Theorizing Engagement: The Potential of a Critical Dialogic Approach." *Accounting, Auditing & Accountability Journal* 20, no. 3 (2007): 356.
14 Michael L. Kent and Maureen Taylor. "Toward a Dialogic Theory of Public Relations." *Public Relations Review* 28, no. 1 (2002): 21–37.
15 Nicholas Browning, "The Ethics of Two-Way Symmetry and the Dilemmas of Dialogic Kantianism." *Journal of Media Ethics* 30, no. 1 (2015): 3.
16 Stefania Romenti, Chiara Valentini, Grazia Murtarelli, and Katia Meggiorin, "Measuring Online Dialogic Conversations' Quality: A Scale Development." *Journal of Communication Management* 20, no. 4 (2016): 328–346.
17 Michael Paquette, Erich J. Sommerfeldt, and Michael L. Kent. "Do the Ends Justify the Means? Dialogue, Development Communication, and Deontological Ethics." *Public Relations Review* 41, no. 1 (2015): 30–39.
18 Ibid.
19 Grant Gross, "Conservative Group Takes Credit for Anti-Net Neutrality Comments." *PC World*, May 11, 2017. www.pcworld.idg.com.au/article/619110/conservative-group-takes-credit-anti-net-neutrality-comments/.
20 Erich J. Sommerfeldt, Michael L. Kent, and Maureen Taylor, "Activist Practitioner Perspectives of Website Public Relations: Why Aren't Activist Websites Fulfilling the Dialogic Promise?" *Public Relations Review* 38, no. 2 (2012): 303–312.

Conclusion

The future of network neutrality is currently in flux. There are many opportunities to overturn the 2017 Federal Communications Commission (FCC) decision to eliminate network neutrality. A majority vote in Congress could block the FCC's rules from going into place, a measure that Representative Doyle seems keen to enact. The FCC could change its mind, citing public interest standards and reversing its own vote. Or, with the election of a new president in 2020, a new Chairperson for the FCC could propose a new set of policies (with the support of other commissioners) that would enact network neutrality again in the United States. Globally, the ramifications for the 2017 decision may be less reversible, as global organizations no longer use network neutrality as the standard-bearer for business decisions.

While the future may be impossible to predict, using the historical impact of dialogic communication on telecommunications policy, three overarching trends present themselves for the future of network neutrality.

As noted in Chapter 6, public engagement in policy development is an ongoing trend demonstrating the value and use of digital dialogic practices. The 2017 Network Neutrality Day of Action merged the interests of activists and large telecommunication organizations to protest the upcoming elimination of the policy. While Chapter 4 questioned the intentions of these organizations, the day resulted in hundreds of protest incidents around the country, as well as the popularization of social media campaigns such as "#SaveTheNet."[1] This merger, between public and private ventures surrounding the network neutrality issue, will continue to evolve, particularly if public support for the policy remains high.

Agnone reflects that a similar trend appeared in the early 2000s regarding environmental reform policies. As consumers became more aware of environmental problems, threats and dangers, consumers began to support policies and organizations that upheld strict environmental protections and standards.[2] Noticing this trend, organizations attempted to align themselves with the growing popularity of the green movement. While many companies did this inauthentically, meaning they only said they supported these initiatives and never changed anti-environmental actions, many organizations did begin to work with consumers and advocacy groups in order to help promote environmental policy changes.[3] Some of the policy changes even held financial implications for the organizations, such as using more costly environmentally friendly materials. To Agnone, organizations did this because they recognized the value of positive public opinion and the benefits of aligning with a popular social cause.[4]

Current partnerships between advocacy groups and large telecommunication organizations seem to mirror the environmental movement of the early 2000s. As the public becomes more aware of network neutrality and demands policies that uphold a free and open internet, large telecommunication organizations are starting to align (even if it is inauthentically) with these interests. Even organizations that recognize the potential financial windfall that may result from eliminating network neutrality are likely to verbalize support for the policy because of the value of public opinion.

Digital dialogic communication drives the perception of public support for network neutrality. The popularity of the #NetNeutrality hashtag, numerous online forums where users vocalize support and even the comments section of online news articles about the policy demonstrate public support for the issue. These digital spaces give organizations insights into popular stances, which are used to inform initiatives such as the partnerships with the Day of Action.

Further, local and state governments have started enforcing individualized network neutrality policies. By March 2018, Montana, New York and New Jersey all proposed policies that would require ISPs who conduct business with the state to uphold network neutrality principles.[5] In announcing the state proposal, Governor Murphy (D-NJ) reflected on the thousands of New Jersey residents who appealed to his office to support network neutrality. While he reflected that the state had limits in its ability to enforce network neutrality, he added that the proposal should "exercise [its] power as a consumer to make [its] preferences known."[6] The New Jersey attorney general also joined a lawsuit filed by a group of states to block the elimination of the policy.

As consumers continue to vocalize support and dissent for network neutrality, there are emerging ways for customers to engage in the public discussion and debate. Increasingly, video and audio appear throughout social media platforms and policy discussions. Rather than singularly typing opinions, consumers are filming or recording their responses. The auditory and visual implications of this richer message exchange provide more information (including nonverbal and paralanguage indicators). In addition, users turn policy content into visual memes, such as Chairman Pai's Harlem Shake dance. These continually emerging forms of expression allow organizations, regulators, political actors and journalists to glean even more information regarding public opinion. While it is not a guarantee that these organizations will use this information when making decisions, it marks a move beyond textual dialogic communication and adds value to the information exchanged in two-way communication. More research is needed on these new forms of digital dialogic communication to understand how the increase in information may impact policy debates and development.

Second, there is increasing interest in examining how organizations respond to changes in regulatory policy. In the aftermath of the FCC's 2017 decision, organizations vocalized support or dissent for the policy decision, many through digital platforms. These responses garnered public feedback through replies, retweets and shares, thus initiating communication. However, many organizations were silent after their initial posting and showed little signs that they took public feedback seriously or integrally. While digitally there was little evidence of the dialogic in these cases, organization's following actions may demonstrate that this feedback did impact organizational decisions and actions. For example, while Comcast vocalized support for the FCC's plans to eliminate network neutrality, they also began an online campaign to illustrate the "non-effect" that the policy's elimination would have on the public. In this case, Comcast did use the information gathered from public feedback, but rather than adjusting its policy or view, it changed its messaging strategy. Months later, Comcast verbalized support for the 2017 Net Neutrality Day of Action, although critics suggest that this was merely to align with a popular issue, not genuine support for the policy.[7]

Measures of authenticity and genuineness in communication are needed in digital dialogic research and could lend themselves to a more theoretical understanding of the illusion of digital dialogic communication. For example, more research is needed to know how the public interpreted Comcast's news release that supported the day of action. Or, for appeals that are criticized as inauthentic, such as Chairman Pai's videos. What indicators does the public use to make this judgment? Throughout the network neutrality debates, there are many actors and organizations who seek to create the illusion of the digital dialogic without actually adhering to the mutual adjustment needed to incorporate feedback. While there are moments of criticism where it seems the public is aware of this illusion, it is unclear what triggers this understanding. It is also likely that the illusion of dialogic communication extends beyond issues of network neutrality. Questions remain regarding the long-term effects of this illusion on organizational or governmental trust and agency.

Finally, although the illusion is present throughout the network neutrality debate, similar questions can be asked about instances where the public perceives authentic dialogic communication. In the case of John Oliver's segment on network neutrality, the public saw his alternative journalism as a mechanism for authentic dialogue. How, in mediated cases, is this digital dialogic conveyed and communicated to the masses? Or, how does alternative journalism motivate public engagement in previously ignored issues?

Although the 2017 FCC decision only directly impacted US internet access, the impact of this policy change extends beyond the region into other continents. Australian citizens reflected that the change in policy could impact business operations in their own country, specifically ones who take their lead from US standards. Or, for some journalists, the move to eliminate network neutrality was one step closer to embodying the free speech censorship that exists in China.

Ongoing is the trend of comparing the US policy to international customs and legal frameworks. This appeared throughout news coverage as well as in the public's own comments toward the issue. These international comparisons seemingly both amplify the demands for change (as if to warn against the cultural context of other regions) and a way to predict how policy changes may impact US business. Comparison appears frequently in digital dialogic communication, and perhaps illustrates the persuasive potential of these instances. More scholarship is needed to examine other persuasive forms of speech occurring in digital dialogic communication.

Federal regulators are far from the only party capable of impacting the network neutrality ruling. Corporations, public advocate groups, media and members of Congress can and have used digital dialogic communication to co-construct policy. As each of these groups uses digital spaces to engage each other, they demonstrate public opinion and motivate the mutual adjustment of perspective and action.

Ultimately, network neutrality is a temporal concept, one that may change at any time based on these ongoing trends. The FCC's decision is not finalized, and even Congressional action or judicial lawsuits can only temporarily reinstate the policy. Just as Chairman Wheeler's 2015 network neutrality ruling was later overturned by Chairman Pai in 2017, future chairpersons can overturn, redefine and regulate large telecommunication organizations using the public interest standards. This temporal nature means that scholars, journalists, organizations, regulators, political actors and members of the public will need to pay attention to the issue for a long time into the future.

Notes

1 Colin Lecher, "Here's How the Internet's Net Neutrality Day of Action Unfolded." *The Verge*, July 12, 2017. www.theverge.com/2017/7/12/15958030/net-neutrality-day-of-action-internet-companies-list.
2 Jon Agnone, "Amplifying Public Opinion: The Policy Impact of the U.S. Environmental Movement." *Social Forces* 85, no. 4 (2007): 1593–1620.
3 Susan M. L. Zee, Sandra J. Hartman, and Lillian Y. Fok, "Commitment to the Green Movement by Organizations and Individuals, Impacts of Organizational Culture, and Perceptions of Impacts upon Outcomes." *International Journal of Applied Management and Technology* 7, no. 1 (2009).
4 Jon Agnone, "Amplifying Public Opinion: The Policy Impact of the U.S. Environmental Movement." *Social Forces* 85, no. 4 (2007): 1593–1620.
5 Mariella Moon, "New Jersey Governor Orders ISPs to Uphold Net Neutrality." *Engadget*, February 2, 2018. www.engadget.com/2018/02/05/new-jersey-order-net-neutrality/.
6 Ibid.
7 David L. Cohen, "Comcast Supports Net Neutrality on the Internet Day of Action." *Comcast*, July 12, 2017. https://corporate.comcast.com/comcast-voices/on-the-internet-day-of-action-comcast-supports-net-neutrality.

Appendix
Methodological Approaches

This book draws upon network neutrality as a case study to examine how digital dialogic practices emerge in debates of public policy. As such, the book draws upon a variety of qualitative methodologies to examine these processes. Methods, datasets and procedures for each of the primary data chapters are described below.

Chapter 2

Ultimately, this chapter sought to answer the following research question: What discourses are used by politicians to describe Net Neutrality and its impact on the public? To answer this question, this project uses a qualitative discourse analysis methodology to examine how politicians described, defined and debated the Net Neutrality issue throughout its multi-year history. To do this, data was collected from the C-SPAN archives from March 1, 1991 to March 1, 2016. This 25-year period reflects the complete mentions of Net Neutrality by politicians. "Net Neutrality" and "network neutrality" were used to collect data, to reflect both spellings. In total, the terms were mentioned 3,545 times by members of Congress during the 25-year period.

To analyze these mentions, the researchers adopted Gee's seven building tasks of discourses to look for recurring themes, terms of reference and definitions of Net Neutrality. Gee's building tasks ask researchers to look at a set of texts as a whole, rather than independent entities. While doing this, researchers look for significance, practices, identities, relationships, politics, connections and sign systems and knowledge. As researchers identify each of these tasks within the set, they also look for recurring themes. In this project, the two researchers read the dataset independently (transcripts and videos) and identified their own set of discourses. After, they discussed the points of similarity and dissimilarity between their discourse sets and rectified any irregularities. For reliability purposes, each discourse is presented with a variety of quotes and examples to support the analysis.

Chapter 3

This chapter looks at the publications and statements issued by members of the Federal Communications Commission (FCC) over a 40-year period. This includes the social media and YouTube accounts of FCC Chairman Pai. Specifically, the chapter looks at how the FCC positions itself within debates over network neutrality. This means examining how it interacts with members of the public and how it responds to public comments within the FCC commenting system. Using discourse analysis, the researchers independently examined a collection of speeches, videos, social media posts and interviews featuring FCC leadership and spokespeople to identify discourses and differences between messaging.

Chapter 4

This chapter builds on the discursive analysis approach from Chapter 3 by investigating how organizations engage in dialogic communication to impact policies on network neutrality. Specifically, it looks at the world's ten largest telecommunication organizations: Comcast Corporation, Walt Disney, Twenty-First Century Fox Inc., Time Warner, Time Warner Cable, DIRECTV, WPP, CBS, Viacom and British Sky Broadcasting. These ten companies control roughly 85% of the world's telecommunication content, including newspapers, television, internet connectivity, mobile and satellites. However, their value and widespread access are greatly dependent upon the regulatory policies that influence their size, scope and reach.

To collect the data, each company's campaigning strategies will be analyzed individually and then collectively. For example, Comcast Corporation issued 15 press releases, eight social media posts (Facebook and Twitter), 28 white papers and three televised commercials on network neutrality. All this content was written and designed for distribution to the public (or media who could distribute it to the public). Because of the variety of platforms, this discursive analysis will look for qualitative patterns and trends amongst each corporation. A set of discourses is identified for each company, then compared across the ten companies to look for differences and similarities in approach, strategy, messaging and audience.

Chapter 5

This chapter reflects on three cases in three types of media coverage (digital, newspapers and television) of network neutrality. First, CNET, arguably one of the first online news organizations dedicated to covering internet and digital technologies, is evaluated for its longitudinal coverage of the topic. This technically oriented site, accessed by millions of users since its 1994 start, has copiously covered network neutrality for 25 years (although it first started calling it network neutrality in 2000). While written for a technically advanced audience, CNET was one of the first digital news platforms to cover issues of network neutrality. Using discourse analysis methods (similarly to Chapters 2 and 3), this section presents a series of discourses that describe how CNET covered network neutrality over time.

Next, the chapter examines newspapers' coverage of network neutrality since 2000 in the ten largest newspapers in the United States. This section reflects on the challenges of making the topic of network neutrality relevant for general readership. It examines the techniques used by journalists to help build understanding of the topic. It also presents institutional biases in the coverage of network neutrality. For example, the *Wall Street Journal* repeatedly frames discussions of network neutrality by reflecting on the policy's business impact (often the negative business impact). However, the *Washington Post* reflects on public access impact rather than business or organizational effect.

Chapter 6

The findings of this chapter are the result of a computer-mediated discourse analysis method. The two authors reviewed 11,400 YouTube comments and analyzed audience engagement. Oliver prompted his viewers at the end of his program to take action and to send comments to the FCC. The YouTube comments revealed how the discourse shaped the issue of media regulation, on a media system owned by one of the largest interactive internet platforms in the world. To do this, discourse analysis of the comments, starting chronologically from the date the program first aired on June 1, 2014, up to May 26, 2015, was conducted. This time period represents the comments added before and after the FCC decision on February 26, 2015. This range was selected because of its ability to demonstrate commenter posts that predict and explain the FCC's decision. As a result, the discourse analysis gives insight into how users react to Oliver's segment, the FCC and Oliver's impact on the regulation.

Specifically, YouTube comments can help identify how an audience engages with a subject, speaker or producer. While studying political debate on YouTube, it is important to identify specific subjects critical to the concepts studied, and then comb through the data to look at how discourses are shaped in relation to the selected topic. For the scope of this project, critical subjects included how the audience reacted to the comedy used to present net neutrality, the reactions to alternative journalism format, and how the audience engages with the larger topic. This chapter is situated as a part of the critical media industry approach as it draws on the framework of scholars who look at the role of power in public discourses.

Index

Printed and bound by CPI Group (UK) Ltd, Croydon, CR0 4YY

24/10/2024

01778282-0003